Gratitude as A Facilitator of Other Virtues in Jehovah God

By Evangeline N. Asafor

© 2019 by Evangeline N. Asafor. All rights reserved. IEM PRESS is honored to present this title with the author. The views expressed or implied in this work are those of the author. No part of this publication may be reproduced, stored in a retrieval system, or transmitted in any way by any means—electronic, mechanical, photocopy, recording, or otherwise—without the prior permission of the copyright holder, except as provided by USA copyright law. Unless otherwise noted, all Scriptures are taken from the Holy Bible, New International Version®, NIV®. Copyright © 1973, 1978, 1984, 2011 by Biblica, Inc.™ Used by permission of Zondervan. All rights reserved worldwide. www.zondervan.com

ISBN 10: 1-947662-43-0

ISBN 13: 978-1-947662-43-8

Library of Congress Catalog Card Number: 2019938574

TABLE OF CONTENTS

INTRODUCTION ....

   Dedication 8
   About the Author 10
   The Importance of Gratitude 11
   The Benefits of Gratitude 13
   The Impact of Gratitude on all Other Virtues 27

CHAPTER ONE: THE VIRTUE OF CHARITY 29

   What is the Virtue of Charity? 29
   What the New International Version of the Bible Says About Charity 30
   Math for the Grateful Soul: Gratitude + Charity = Graticharitude 34
   Great Quotes On Gratitude And Charity 35
   The Emotional Benefits of Charity and Gratitude 36
   The Health Benefits of Charity and Gratitude 37
   The Career Benefits of Charity and Gratitude 37
   The Social Benefits of Charity and Gratitude 37
   The Personality Benefits of Charity and Gratitude 38
   Math for the Ungrateful Soul: Charity - Gratitude = Greed 38
   What the New International Version of the Bible Says About Greed 39

CHAPTER TWO: THE VIRTUE OF CHASTITY 41

   What is the Virtue of Chastity? 41

Math for the Grateful Soul: Gratitude + Chastity = Gratichastitude 42
The Benefits of Chastity Before Marriage 43
What the New International Version of the Bible Says about Chastity 43
Great Quotes on Chastity.. 45
Math for the Ungrateful Soul: Chastity - Gratitude = lust........... 46
What the New International Version of the Bible Says about lust 47

CHAPTER THREE: THE VIRTUE DILIGENCE............ 50

What is the Virtue of Diligence? 50
What the New International Version of the Bible Says About Diligence.. 51
What Some Great Minds Say About Diligence 53
Math for the Grateful Soul: Gratitude + Diligence = Gratidiligenitude.. 54
Math for the Ungrateful Soul: Diligence - Gratitude = Sloth...... 55
What the New International Version of the Bible Says About Sloth 56

CHAPTER FOUR: THE VIRTUE OF FAITH.................. 59

What is the Virtue of Faith?... 59
What the New International Version of the Bible Says About Faith... 60
Some Luminary Members of the Hebrew Hall of Faith 61
Types of Faith 64
Steps to Grow Your Faith 65
What Some Great Minds Say About Faith in God 66
Math for the Grateful Soul: Gratitude + Faith = Gratifaithitude 67
Math for the Ungrateful Soul: Faith - Gratitude = Fear.............. 68
What the New International Version of the Bible Says About Fear.. 69

What Nelson Mandela Says About Fear 71

CHAPTER FIVE: THE VIRTUE OF FORTITUDE 73

What is the Virtue of Fortitude? 73
What the New International Version of the Bible Says About Fortitude 73
What Some Great Minds Say About Fortitude 74
Math for the Grateful Soul: Gratitude + Fortitude = Gratifortitude 75
Math for the Ungrateful Soul: Fortitude − Gratitude = Faintheartedness 76
What the New International Version of the Bible Says About Faintheartedness 76
What Some Great Minds Say About Faintheartedness 78

CHAPTER SIX: THE VIRTUE OF HUMILITY 80

What is the Virtue of Humility? 80
What the New International Version of the Bible Says About Humility 81
What Some Great Minds Say About Humility 84
Twelve Ways to Humble Yourself by Billy Graham 89
Math for the Grateful Soul: Gratitude + Humility = Gratihumilitude 92
Math for the Ungrateful Soul: Humility − Gratitude = Pride 93
What the New International Version of the Bible Says About Pride 93

CHAPTER SEVEN: THE VIRTUE OF JUSTICE 95

What is the Virtue of Justice? 95
What the New International Version of the Bible Says About Justice 96
What Some Great Minds Say About Justice 97

Math for the Grateful Soul: Gratitude + Justice = Gratijustitude 98
Math for the Ungrateful Soul: Justice − Gratitude = Injustice 99
What the New Version of the Holy Bible Says about Injustice .99

CHAPTER EIGHT: THE VIRTUE OF PATIENCE 102

What is the Virtue of Patience? 102
What the New International Version of the Bible Says about Patience 102
What Some Great Minds Say About Patience 103
Math for the Grateful Soul: Gratitude + Patience = Gratipatienitude...105
Math for the Ungrateful Soul: Patience − Gratitude = Wrath ..105
What the New International Version of the Holy Bible Says about Wrath 105

CHAPTER NINE: THE VIRTUE OF PRUDENCE 108

What is the Virtue of Prudence? 108
What the New International Version of the Bible Says about Prudence 109
What Some Great Minds Say About Prudence 110
Math for the Grateful Soul: Gratitude + Prudence = Gratiprudenitude...110
Math for the Ungrateful Soul: Prudence − Gratitude = Folly ...111
What the New International Version of the Bible Says About Folly 111

CHAPTER TEN: THE VIRTUE OF TEMPERANCE 114

What is the Virtue of Temperance? 114
What the New International Version of the Bible Says About Temperance 115
What Some Great Minds Say About Temperance 119
Math for the Grateful Soul: Gratitude + Temperance= Gratitemperitude...122

Math for the Ungrateful Soul: Temperance – Gratitude = Gluttony 122
What the New International Version of the Bible Says About Gluttony 123

CONCLUSION 125

Show Gratitude for the Uplifting Grace of Jehovah God 125
What the New International Version of the Bible Says About Grace 127
What the Luminary Dr. Mensah Otabil Says About Grace 130
What Some Great Minds Say About God's Uplifting Grace ... 131

REVIEWS 135

DEDICATION

When I think of gratitude, I cannot thank Jehovah God enough for entrusting me with four of HIS most treasured creations. With a humble spirit and a grateful heart, I dedicate this book to my fearfully and wonderfully made offspring; Angela (My Angel), Tiffany (My Treasure), Bryan (My Blessing) and Ryan (My Riches). May Jehovah God continue to bless, protect, and guide them as they continue to seek his kingdom and his righteousness.

ABOUT THE AUTHOR

Evangeline N. Asafor is originally from Cameroon near the west coast of Central Africa. As a little girl growing up, she had a dream of one day becoming an international agent of social change—a dream she thought her native country could not contain. So, she migrated to the United States of America in October of 2000. One of her best days in America was the day she was sworn in as a US citizen! She made a promise to herself to be an asset to this great nation, not a liability.

Evangeline has published two inspirational Books in her "Gratitude Series" entitled; "My letters of Gratitude to Jehovah, God" and "My SweetMother's Doctrines of Gratitude and her Final Rest with Jehovah, God." Evangeline loves motherhood, reading, writing, researching, coaching, mentoring, evangelizing and travelling.

One of her significant spiritual growth moments happened when her Godly-Ordained life coach and Spiritual Director recommended the teachings of Dr. Mensa Otabil to her. After listening to about ten of his sermons on Utube, her prayer focus changed from "Lord Teach me wisdom" to "Help me to seek thy kingdom and Thy Righteousness oh God" this change of prayer focus has and continues to transform Evangeline day after day as she hungers and thirsts for righteousness. May Jehovah God continue to bless, inspire and equip Dr. Otabil as he continues to be a great Steward to the multitudes nationwide.

THE IMPORTANCE OF GRATITUDE

Gratitude as a virtue is very significant in facilitating other virtues like Chastity, Charity, Diligence, Faith, Fortitude, Humility, Justice, Patience, Prudence, Temperance, and must be given the attention that it deserves. Gratitude is the quality of being thankful, readiness to show appreciation for and to return kindness. When gratitude is added as an ingredient to other virtues, it can increasingly benefit the soul and channel it to hunger and thirst for righteousness.

Gratefulness, feeling or showing an appreciation of kindness; thankful.
Recognition, acknowledgment of something's existence, validity, or legality.
Appreciativeness, feeling or showing gratitude or pleasure.
Thankfulness, expressing gratitude and relief
Indebtedness, the feeling of owing gratitude for a service or favor.
Teachability, Able and grateful to learn God's Love and insights by being taught
Understanding, having insight or good judgment.
Devotedness, a state of being faithful
Enthusiasm, intense and eager enjoyment, interest, or approval.

Gratitude is a vital virtue that can lead to overall happiness by enhancing emotional wellbeing, an individual's personality, overall health, career, as well as social life (AMIT, AMIN). The following 31 benefits of gratitude came about because of more than 40 research studies on Gratitude; Reference is as follows;

Date & Journal: 1988, British Journal of Social Psychology
Authors: Shula Sommers and Corinne Kosmitzki
Sample size: 105 American and 40 German adults

THE BENEFITS OF GRATITUDE

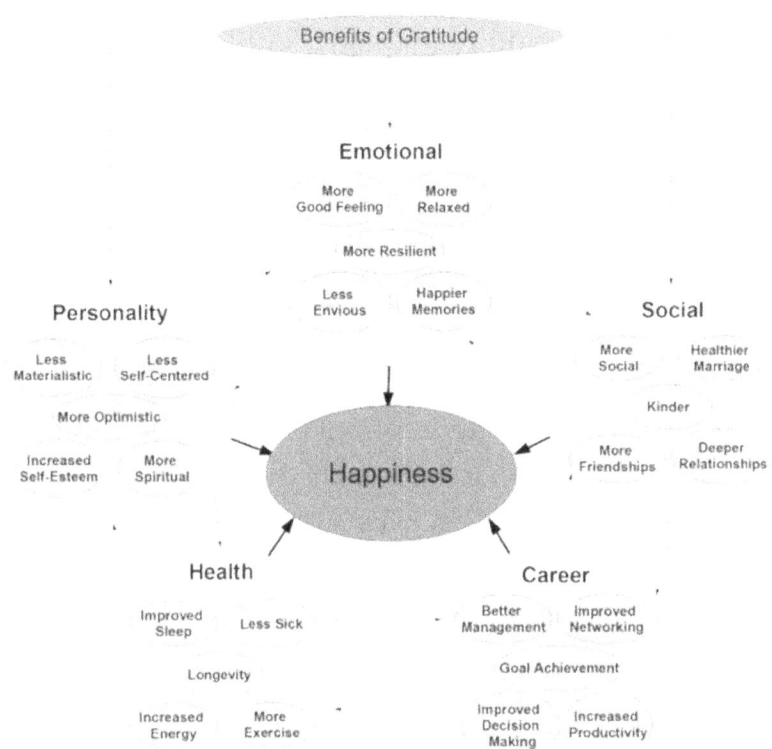

In todays complicated and ever-changing world, every one of Jehovah's creations need an attitude of gratitude with gratitude playing in every heart and on every lip to be able to overcome the enemy's lies.

An attitude of gratitude will enable any servant of Jehovah most high to stay strong even when they feel weak, not to faint in the face of adversity, to have a forward focus to pursue Godly ordained dreams even when the way forward Looks Blocked. An attitude of gratitude will enable any follower of Jehovah most high to be strong in the Lord and in the power of his might by constantly speaking Jehovah God's words into any situation. With an attitude of gratitude, all may seem lost, but the Grace of Jehovah God will abound and enable any faithful servant to pursue, overtake, and recover all what was deemed lost.

Jehovah, God who sees in secret will reward any Christian openly when they fast and pray with an attitude of gratitude (Mathew 6:6). An attitude of gratitude to Jehovah God will enable a Christian to fast and develop spiritual hunger for God showing God what is in his or her heart. An attitude of gratitude to Jehovah God will enable a Christian to live and multiply. An attitude of gratitude to Jehovah God will enable a Christian to appreciate the fact that man does not live by bread alone but by every word that proceeds from the mouth of God (Mathew 4:4).

The joy of Jehovah God will provide strength to his anointed and chosen ones when we come to him with praise and thanksgiving. An attitude of gratitude will enable Jehovah God's children in the name of Jesus his begotten son to possess one's soul from fear, hatred, bitterness, negativity and unforgiveness. An attitude of gratitude will enable believers to stay their minds on Jehovah God and come to him anytime in the name of his son Jesus, Christ and be kept in perfect peace. In every problem and messy situation, as a child of Jehovah God most high, in the name of Jesus Christ, any believer will be able to make a way out and turn the mess into a message of empowerment for others.

When any believer or servant of Jehovah God most high comes to him in the name of Jesus Christ, Jehovah will prepare a table for him even in the presence of his enemies and anoint his head with oil (Psalm 23). In any believer's day of distress, if they call unto Jehovah God in the name of Jesus Christ with an attitude of gratitude, Jehovah God will rescue them, and all he asks in return is for his name to be glorified (Psalm 50:15). When you come to Jehovah God in the name of his son Jesus Christ, you will find whatever you are seeking, the doors will be opened to you when you knock, and you will be given whatever you are asking according to your Godly ordained purpose as designed by Jehovah God (Mathew 7:7). When you call unto Jehovah God with an attitude of gratitude in the name of Jesus Christ, Jehovah will enable you to seize opportunities of a life time during the life time of those opportunities in the abled leadership of the holy spirit.

In the name of Jesus Christ, even if one door of happiness closes in Jehovah God's servant's face, Jehovah will make sure other doors of happiness are available for you to jump into with an attitude of gratitude. Gratitude to Jehovah God will enable your outward actions to match your inward discipline. Having an attitude of gratitude towards Jehovah God will enable one to create a better future by defying reality and pursuing one's Godly ordained purpose on this earth. Showing gratitude to Jehovah God can enable one to fully understand that God has not given him/her the spirit of negative fear (False Emotions Appearing as Real) but the positive spirits of power, love and a sound mind (2 Timothy 1:7). An attitude of gratitude can enable one to stay strong even when they feel weak. With an attitude of gratitude towards Jehovah God whoever hungers and thirst for righteousness will be blessed and filled with righteousness (Mathew 5:6). An attitude of gratitude will help transform a life into a legacy and enable one to find peace in times of trouble (Psalm 3). Gratitude is the healthiest of all human emotions, and the more you express gratitude for what you have, the more likely you will have even more to express gratitude for (Zig Ziglar).

The importance of gratitude as a virtue that makes other virtues possible cannot be over emphasized, it's the main ingredient in the soup for the soul by the grace of Jehovah God and in the name of his son Jesus Christ. Gratitude will enable any believer in Jehovah God to see God in the middle of ALL their storms. An attitude of gratitude will enable any believer to walk in faith and not by sight, enabling such a believer to be less aware of the storm and more aware of the mighty presence of God in that storm. Gratitude will enable any believer to carry a crown before they can wear one, thus enabling them to serve their way up to greatness and success. An attitude of gratitude will enable any believer to believe in themselves that they can do all things through Christ who strengthens them (Philippines 4:13). An attitude of gratitude will enable any believer in Jehovah God to use the measure of faith given to them by God to move mountains and still not think of themselves higher than they ought to think (Romans 12:3). An attitude of gratitude will inspire every believer in Jehovah God to magnify, glorify, sanctify, edify and testify God. An attitude of gratitude will enable believers to be still and know that God is above all the trials and have everyone of his creations in the palms of his hand. With an attitude of gratitude, it becomes easier to live out of a place pf peace and trust that Jehovah God will do what he says he will do. An attitude of gratitude to Jehovah God will enable God to turn your ashes into beauty any time, any where and as many times as he deems fit. When you appreciate all Jehovah God has already done in your life, that attitude of gratitude will enable you to see God's concern into everything that concerns you, and be at peace knowing he, the almighty will do again and again what he did for you in the past. An attitude of gratitude will fuel your measure of faith and make you experience the mighty power of God.

An attitude of gratitude will enable you as a believer in Jehovah God and his son Jesus, not to get weary in well doing. And consequently, Jehovah God will not only bless you despite your opposition but will bless you in front of your opposition (Psalm 23:5). An attitude of gratitude will enable you to encourage yourself into victory, strength, and favor so that it will be easier for Jehovah God to accompany your vision with provision at the appropriate time according to the riches of his glory in Christ Jesus (Philippians 4:19). An attitude of gratitude will enable you to consistently anchor to hope towards your Godly ordained destiny and enable Jehovah God to reverse and restore you and keep you from drifting away. Showing Jehovah God gratitude continually will reveal the truth about him that he is all powerful and exceeds expectations and is able to do exceedingly above all that we can ask or think (Ephesians 3:20). With an attitude of gratitude, your disability becomes your purpose and your test becomes your testimony.

With an attitude of gratitude, you will be able to view your setbacks as setups for God to work in your life. Be a prisoner of hope and Jehovah God, will pay you back double. You will be able to better appreciate Jehovah God's protection, direction and correction when you cultivate and maintain an attitude of gratitude. You will be strengthened and inspired to look down to your problems and look up with hope to Jehovah, God for your solutions.

An attitude of gratitude will enable Jehovah God to lead you to the hidden treasures in secret places at the appointed time and opportunity. An attitude of gratitude will strengthen you to do what you can, so God can do for you what you can't do for yourself.

An attitude of gratitude will enable you to seize opportunities of a lifetime during the lifespan of such opportunities. An attitude of gratitude will enable you to radically obey Jehovah God for Radical blessings in return that will enable you to consistently anchor to hope and not drift away from your Godly ordained destiny. An attitude of gratitude will enable you use your disability as your purpose and use your test as your testimony. It will reveal to you the God who exceeds expectations and is able to do exceedingly above all that we can ask or think (Ephesians 3:20).

An attitude of gratitude will keep a believer focused on Jesus so that the holy spirit can go to work in the favor of such a believer.

Show love and trust to Jehovah God and his son Jesus Christ by living life with an attitude of gratitude for what he has done, what he is doing and what he will do. An attitude of gratitude will enable Jehovah God to open doors that no man can open, and to close doors that no man can reopen.

When you kiss your pass goodbye and focus on Jehovah God and his promises with an attitude of gratitude, Jehovah God abundantly blesses your future.

When you cultivate and live a life of gratitude, Jehovah God will work out his promises for your life and make your seeds to flourish wherever they are planted.

An attitude of gratitude will enable far out things to chase you down, opportunities will come knocking, favor will be your portion. When you give Jehovah God an attitude of gratitude by praising him even in times of difficulties, the walls will come tumbling before your own very eyes like the walls of Jericho (Joshua 6:1-27).

> *Joshua 6:1-27:* "Now the gates of Jericho were securely barred because of the Israelites. No one went out and no one came in. Then the LORD said to Joshua, "See, I have delivered Jericho into your hands, along with its king and its fighting men. March around the city once with all the armed men. Do this for six days. Have seven priests carry trumpets of rams' horns in front of the ark. On the seventh day, march around the city seven times, with the priests blowing the trumpets. When you hear them sound a long blast on the trumpets, have the whole army give a loud shout; then the wall of the city will collapse and the army will go up, everyone straight in."
>
> So, Joshua son of Nun called the priests and said to them, "Take up the ark of the covenant of the LORD and have seven priests carry trumpets in front of it." And he ordered the army, "Advance! March around

the city, with an armed guard going ahead of the ark of the Lord."

When Joshua had spoken to the people, the seven priests carrying the seven trumpets before the Lord went forward, blowing their trumpets, and the ark of the Lord's covenant followed them. The armed guard marched ahead of the priests who blew the trumpets, and the rear guard followed the ark. All this time the trumpets were sounding. But Joshua had commanded the army, "Do not give a war cry, do not raise your voices, do not say a word until the day I tell you to shout. Then shout!" [11] So he had the ark of the Lord carried around the city, circling it once. Then the army returned to camp and spent the night there.

Joshua got up early the next morning and the priests took up the ark of the Lord. The seven priests carrying the seven trumpets went forward, marching before the ark of the Lord and blowing the trumpets. The armed men went ahead of them and the rear guard followed the ark of the Lord, while the trumpets kept sounding. So, on the second day they marched around the city once and returned to the camp. They did this for six days.

On the seventh day, they got up at daybreak and marched around the city seven times in the same manner, except that on that day they circled the city seven times. The seventh time around, when the priests sounded the trumpet blast, Joshua commanded the army, "Shout! For the LORD has given you the city! The city and all that is in it are to be devoted to the LORD. Only Rahab the prostitute and all who are with her in her house shall be spared, because she hid the spies we sent. But keep away from the devoted things, so that you will not bring about your own destruction by taking any of them. Otherwise you will make the camp of Israel liable to destruction and bring trouble on it. All the silver and gold and the articles of bronze and iron are sacred to the LORD and must go into his treasury."

When the trumpets sounded, the army shouted, and at the sound of the trumpet, when the men gave a loud shout, the wall collapsed; so, everyone charged straight in, and they took the city. They devoted the city to the LORD and destroyed with the sword every living thing in it—men and women, young and old, cattle, sheep and donkeys.

Joshua said to the two men who had spied out the land, "Go into the prostitute's house and bring her out and all who belong to her, in accordance with your oath to her." So, the young men who had done the spying went in and brought out Rahab, her father and mother, her brothers and sisters and all who belonged to her. They brought out her entire family and put them in a place outside the camp of Israel.

Then they burned the whole city and everything in it, but they put the silver and gold and the articles of bronze and iron into the treasury of the LORD's house. But Joshua spared Rahab the prostitute, with her family and all who belonged to her, because she hid the men Joshua had sent as spies to Jericho—and she lives among the Israelites to this day.

At that time Joshua pronounced this solemn oath: "Cursed before the LORD is the one who undertakes to rebuild this city, Jericho: "At the cost of his firstborn son he will lay its foundations; at the cost of his youngest he will set up its gates." So, the LORD was with Joshua, and his fame spread throughout the land.

David the sweet psalmist of Israel and his attitude of gratitude towards Jehovah God enabled him to conquer a giant with a simple sling shot.

1Samuel 17:48-50: As the Philistine moved closer to attack him, David ran quickly toward the battle line to meet him. Reaching into his bag and taking out a stone, he slung it and struck the Philistine on the forehead. The stone sank into his forehead, and he fell face down on the ground. So, David triumphed over the Philistine with a sling and a stone; without a sword in his hand he struck down the Philistine and killed him.

Psalm 16:8-9: "I keep my eyes always on the LORD. With him at my right hand, I will not be shaken. Therefore, my heart is glad, and my tongue rejoices; my body also." David was not perfect in any sense but was focused on God and his promises with an attitude of gratitude.

The Effect of Gratitude on the Gifts of the Holy Spirit

An attitude of gratitude + the gifts of the Holy Spirit = The fruits of the Holy Spirit

An attitude of gratitude will enable believers to understand the difference between the gifts of the Holy Spirit and the fruits of the Holy Spirit.

The **Fruit of the Holy Spirit** is a biblical term that sums up nine attributes of a person or community living in accord with the Holy Spirit, according to chapter 5 of the Epistle to the Galatians: "But the fruit of the Spirit is love, joy, peace, patience, kindness, goodness, faithfulness, gentleness, and self-control."(Galatians 5:22, KJV).

The **Seven gifts of the Holy Spirit** are found in the book of Isiah Chapter 11 in verses 2 and 3. "The Spirit of the Lord will rest on him— the Spirit of wisdom and of understanding, the Spirit of counsel and of might, the Spirit of the knowledge and fear of the Lord— and he will delight in the fear of the Lord. He will not judge by what he sees with his eyes or decide by what he hears with his ears;" (Isiah 11:2-3, NIV).

The seven gifts of the holy spirit according to the Book of Isiah are: wisdom, understanding, counsel, fortitude, knowledge, piety, and fear of the Lord. An attitude of gratitude will help you cultivate the fruits of the Holy Spirit, and the fruits of the Holy Spirit will in turn help you regulate the gifts of the Holy Spirit.

Once you know the difference between the fruits of the holy spirit and the gifts of the holy spirit, its important to know how to receive, grow and protect these Godly assets. The 1st Book of Corinthians:

"Now about the gifts of the Spirit, brothers and sisters, I do not want you to be uninformed. You know that when you were pagans, somehow or other you were influenced and led astray to mute idols. Therefore, I want you to know that no one who is speaking by the Spirit of God says, "Jesus be cursed," and no one can say, "Jesus is Lord," except by the Holy Spirit. There are different kinds of gifts, but the same Spirit distributes them. There are different kinds of service, but the same Lord. There are different kinds of working, but in all of them and in everyone it is the same God at work. Now to each one the manifestation of the Spirit is given for the common good. To one there is given through the Spirit a message of wisdom, to another a message of knowledge by means of the same Spirit, to another faith by the same Spirit, to another gifts of healing by that one Spirit, to another miraculous powers, to another prophecy, to another distinguishing between spirits, to another speaking in different kinds of tongues, and to still another the interpretation of tongues. All these are the work of one and the same Spirit, and he distributes them to each one, just as he determines." *(1st Corinthians 12: 1-11, NIV)*.

Cultivating and maintaining an attitude of gratitude will constantly remind you that though your destiny is chosen by God, fulfilling it is your decision. As a child of Jehovah God almighty, your future is certain and it's a good one, but whether you arrive there is pretty much up to you. The mountains don't get bigger, but your faith can grow and defeat the mountains in your life when you cultivate and maintain an attitude of gratitude. An attitude of gratitude reminds you that

1. your future existed before your present,
2. your future is God's past, your future is the end trapped in the beginning,
3. God is committed in the future he placed in you
4. your future is greater than your past,
5. what is around you, is not as important as what is in you (greater is he who is in you, than he who is in the world)
6. Jesus forgave your past, so that he can salvage your future.

We normally meet our destiny casually under obedience of authority with an attitude of gratitude. This can occur when we obey simple instructions such as the one David obeyed from his father Jesse "Take this ephah of roasted grain and these ten loaves of bread for your brothers and hurry to their camp." *(1 Samuel 17:17, NIV).*

In love God predestined you with every spiritual blessing needed for your future ordained purpose. Your future is more powerful than your mistakes and pressure is an incubator for success when you cultivate and maintain an attitude of gratitude. A grateful heart as described by James E. Faust is a beginning of greatness. It is an expression of humility. It is a foundation for the development of such virtues as prayer, faith, courage, contentment, happiness, love, and well-being.

Ingratitude on the other hand refers to a lack of appreciation towards Jehovah God and all what he has created. Ingratitude is engrained in the following vices; lust, greed, sloth, mistrust, faintheartedness, pride, injustice, wrath, folly and gluttony. In the case of Adam and Eve in the garden of Eden, their ingratitude was wrapped up in the vices of greed, sloth, mistrust, faintheartedness, gluttony, pride and folly. The first Original sin committed by Adam and Eve in the Garden of Eden was that of Ingratitude (Genesis Chapter 2). The desire for more that made Adam and Eve vulnerable to the serpent's attack in the Garden of Eden was fueled by **ingratitude, they were not satisfied with the glory of life God happily and willingly gave them (Genesis Chapter 2)**

THE IMPACT OF GRATITUDE ON ALL OTHER VIRTUES

An attitude of Gratitude to Jehovah God enables the WUK (Wisdom, Understanding and Knowledge) of Charity, Chastity, Diligence, Faith, Fortitude, Humility, Justice, Patience, Prudence, and Temperance.

Cultivating and maintaining an attitude of Gratitude furthers the Virtue of Charity

Cultivating and maintaining an attitude of Gratitude fortifies the Virtue of Chastity

Cultivating and maintaining an attitude of Gratitude enables the Virtue of Diligence

Cultivating and maintaining an attitude of Gratitude expediates the Virtue of Faith

Cultivating and maintaining an attitude of Gratitude eases the Virtue of Fortitude

Cultivating and maintaining an attitude of Gratitude facilitates the Virtue of Humility

Cultivating and maintaining an attitude of Gratitude enhances the Virtue of Justice

Cultivating and maintaining an attitude of Gratitude reinforces the Virtue of Patience

Cultivating and maintaining an attitude of Gratitude inspires the Virtue of Prudence

Cultivating and upholding an attitude of Gratitude boosts the Virtue of Temperance

CHAPTER ONE:
THE VIRTUE OF CHARITY

What is the Virtue of Charity?

Compassion towards others
Honoring others
Altruism towards others
Respecting others
Impacting the lives of others in a positive way
Tolerance in judging others.
Yielding to God's plan and purpose for your life

Charity refers to generosity and helpfulness towards the needy or those suffering. Charity is best practiced when one cultivates an attitude of gratitude. Being unconditionally grateful is a catalyst for doing charitable deeds and thus changing lives. Gratitude as a foundational virtue upon which happiness and spiritual growth depends makes it easy for one to reach out to the needy or those suffering. Reaching out to those in need helps one to better appreciate one's life and it also unshackles one from toxic emotions. "The greatness of a man is measured by the way he treats the little man. Compassion for the weak is a sign of greatness."
- Myles Munroe

What the New International Version of the Bible Says About Charity

1. ***Acts 20:35*** – "In everything I did, I showed you that by this kind of hard work we must help the weak, remembering the words the LORD Jesus himself said: 'It is more blessed to give than to receive.'"

2. ***Hebrews 13:16*** – "And do not forget to do good and to share with others, for with such sacrifices God is pleased."

3. ***Galatians 6:9***. "Let us not become weary in doing good, for at the proper time we will reap a harvest if we do not give up."

4. ***Matthew 5:42*** – "Give to the one who asks you, and do not turn away from the one who wants to borrow from you."

5. ***Matthew 6:1-4*** - Be careful not to practice your righteousness in front of others to be seen by them. If you do, you will have no reward from your Father in heaven. So, when you give to the needy, do not announce it with trumpets, as the hypocrites do in the synagogues and on the streets, to be honored by others. Truly I tell you, they have received their reward in full. But when you give to the needy, do not let your left hand know what your right hand is doing, so that your giving may be in secret. Then your Father, who sees what is done in secret, will reward you.

6. ***Mathew 25:35-40***. "For I was hungry and you gave me something to eat, I was thirsty and you gave me

something to drink, I was a stranger and you invited me in, I needed clothes and you clothed me, I was sick and you looked after me, I was in prison and you came to visit me.' Then the righteous will answer him, 'Lord, when did we see you hungry and feed you, or thirsty and give you something to drink? When did we see you a stranger and invite you in, or needing clothes and clothe you? When did we see you sick or in prison and go to visit you?' "The King will reply, 'Truly I tell you, whatever you did for one of the least of these brothers and sisters of mine, you did for me.'

7. ***Luke 6:35***. *"But* love your enemies, do good to them, and lend to them without expecting to get anything back. Then your reward will be great, and you will be children of the Highest, because he is kind to the ungrateful and wicked."

8. ***Luke 6:38*** – "Give, and it will be given to you. A good measure, pressed down, shaken together and running over, will be poured into your lap. For with the measure you use, it will be measured to you."

9. ***Luke 10:35***. "The next day he took out two denarii and gave them to the innkeeper. 'Look after him,' he said, 'and when I return, I will reimburse you for any extra expense you may have."

10. ***Luke 12:33*** – "Sell your possessions and give to the poor. Provide purses for yourselves that will not wear out, a treasure in heaven that will never fail, where no thief comes near, and no moth destroys."

11. ***Luke 14: 13-14****.* "But when you give a banquet, invite the poor, the crippled, the lame, the blind, and you will be blessed. Although they cannot repay you, you will be repaid at the resurrection of the righteous."

12. ***Luke 18:22****.* "When Jesus heard this, he said to him, "You still lack one thing. Sell everything you have and give to the poor, and you will have treasure in heaven. Then come, follow me."

13. ***Luke 21:1-4*** - As Jesus looked up, he saw the rich putting their gifts into the temple treasury. He also saw a poor widow put in two very small copper coins. Truly I tell you," he said, "this poor widow has put in more than all the others. All these people gave their gifts out of their wealth; but she out of her poverty put in all she had to live on."

14. ***I Corinthians 9: 6-7****.* Remember this: Whoever sows sparingly will also reap sparingly, and whoever sows generously will also reap generously. Each of you should give what you have decided in your heart to give, not reluctantly or under compulsion, for God loves a cheerful giver."

15. ***2 Corinthians 9:7*** – "Each of you should give what you have decided in your heart to give, not reluctantly or under compulsion, for God loves a cheerful giver."

16. ***Proverbs 19:17*** – "Whoever is kind to the poor lends to the LORD, and he will reward them for what they have done."

17. *1 John 3:17* – "If anyone has material possessions and sees a brother or sister in need but has no pity on them, how can the love of God be in that person?"

18. *Deuteronomy 15:7-11* - If anyone is poor among your fellow Israelites in any of the towns of the land the LORD your God is giving you, do not be hardhearted or tightfisted toward them. Rather, be openhanded and freely lend them whatever they need. Be careful not to harbor this wicked thought: "The seventh year, the year for canceling debts, is near," so that you do not show ill will toward the needy among your fellow Israelites and give them nothing. They may then appeal to the LORD against you, and you will be found guilty of sin. Give generously to them and do so without a grudging heart; then because of this the LORD your God will bless you in all your work and in everything you put your hand to. There will always be poor people in the land. Therefore, I command you to be openhanded toward your fellow Israelites who are poor and needy in your land.

19. *Hebrews 13:2* – "Do not forget to show hospitality to strangers, for by so doing some people have shown hospitality to angels without knowing it."

20. *Proverbs 21:13* – "Whoever shuts their ears to the cry of the poor will also cry out and not be answered."

21. *Psalms 112: 5-9*. "Good will come to those who are generous and lend freely, who conduct their affairs with justice. Surely the righteous will never be shaken; they will be remembered forever. They will

have no fear of bad news; their hearts are steadfast, trusting in the LORD. Their hearts are secure, they will have no fear; in the end they will look in triumph on their foes. They have freely scattered their gifts to the poor, their righteousness endures forever; their horn will be lifted high in honor."

22. *Isaiah 58:10.* "And if you spend yourselves in behalf of the hungry and satisfy the needs of the oppressed, then your light will rise in the darkness, and your night will become like the noonday."

Math for the Grateful Soul: Gratitude + Charity = Graticharitude

Gratefulness
Recognition
Appreciation
Thankfulness
Indebtedness
Compassion
Honor
Altruism
Respect
Impact
Tolerance
Understanding
Devotedness
Enthusiasm

Graticharitude refers to the quality of being thankful and the readiness to show appreciation to Jehovah God through sacrifice, generosity or benevolence. Graticharitude enables you to be a rainbow in another person's cloud (Maya Angelou). Graticharitude makes it possible for an individual to become an anchor in another one's life ocean (Don Williams). With an attitude of Graticharitude, you can become a catalyst in other people's life reactions. Graticharitude enables you to be a valuable piece in another person's life puzzle.

GREAT QUOTES ON GRATITUDE AND CHARITY (GRATICHARITUDE)

- "Love is not patronizing, and charity isn't about pity, it is about love. Charity and love are the same -- with charity you give love, so don't just give money but reach out your hand instead. It's not how much we give but how much love we put into giving." ~ **Mother Theresa**
- "A life not lived for others is not a life." ~**Mother Teresa**
- "We make a living by what we get, but we make a life by what we give." ~ **Winston Churchill**
- "Charity begins at home but should not end there." ~**Thomas Fuller**
- "Charity is not a duty but a joy." ~**Joseph W. Sitati**
- "Real Charity is giving from the heart without taking credit." ~**Michael Jackson**

- "Associate yourself with the poor and the needy; be friendly with them and sit in their company." ~ **_Prophet Muhammad_**
- "Real Charity is not something you give away; it is something that you acquire and make a part of yourself. And when the virtue of charity becomes implanted in your heart, you are never the same again." ~ **_Marvin J. Ashton_**
- "The best way to find yourself is to lose yourself in the service of others." ~ **_Mahatma Gandhi_**
- "Volunteers do not necessarily have the time; they just have the heart." ~**_Elizabeth Andrew_**
- "Gratitude and charity are the secret essence to finding our inner life force, the divine energy." ~ **_Deborah Bee_**
- "Not everybody can be famous, but everybody can be great, because greatness is determined by service." ~ **_Martin Luther King Jr._**

The Emotional Benefits of Charity and Gratitude (Graticharitude)

The emotional benefits of being thankful and the readiness to show appreciation to Jehovah God through sacrifice, generosity or benevolence are many. One will generally have a good feeling, feel more relaxed, have more resilience, become less envious and cultivate happier memories when they show appreciation to Jehovah God by reaching out to those in need.

The Health Benefits of Charity and Gratitude (Graticharitude)

There are many health benefits of being thankful and enthusiastic as a sign of gratitude to Jehovah God through sacrifice, generosity or benevolence. An individual in a Graticharitude state will generally have improved sleep, become less sick, experience increased energy, and a greater potential for longevity.

The Career Benefits of Charity and Gratitude (Graticharitude)

There are some career benefits of being thankful and enthusiastic as a sign of gratitude to Jehovah God through sacrifice, generosity or benevolence worth noting. An individual in a Graticharitude state will generally have better management skills, improved networking skills, improved decision-making skills, and increased productivity. A Graticharitude state will positively impact Moral courage, Emotional Courage, Social Courage, Physical Courage, Intellectual Courage, Spiritual Courage as a great leadership tool that enables leaders to lead with moral, emotional, Social physical, intellectual and spiritual authority.

The Social Benefits of Charity and Gratitude (Graticharitude)

There are some social benefits of being thankful and enthusiastic as a sign of gratitude to Jehovah God through sacrifice, generosity or benevolence worth noting. An individual in a Graticharitude state will generally have more social skills, social courage, healthier marriages, deeper relationships, more friendships, and increased kindness. under the anointing of Graticharitude it becomes possible for the youths to lead and never too late for the old to learn. No one under the anointing of Graticharitude will want to trade their worst day in life for anyone's best day in life. People under the anointing of Graticharitude don't get jealous when others succeed, they get curious when they see success. People under the anointing of Graticharitude don't talk or play with their cellphones while on the table with family or friends

The Personality Benefits of Charity and Gratitude (Graticharitude)

There are some personality benefits of being thankful and enthusiastic as a sign of gratitude to Jehovah God through sacrifice, generosity or benevolence worth noting. An individual in a Graticharitude state will generally be less materialistic, less self-centered, more optimistic, increased self-esteem, and more spiritual.

Math for the Ungrateful Soul: Charity - Gratitude = Greed

Greed refers to an intense and selfish desire for something, especially wealth, power, or food.

Whenever we fail to show generosity and helpfulness towards the needy or those suffering, we become greedy in the eyes of Jehovah God and we cultivate ungrateful souls. Our maker Jehovah God does not only require us to show charity but appreciates it more if we give cheerfully (2 Corinthians

9:7). An attitude of gratitude makes it easier to give cheerfully as Jehovah God commands through his Son Jesus Christ.

What the New International Version of the Holy Bible Says About Greed

1. ***1 Corinthians 6:10*** – "nor thieves, nor the greedy, nor drunkards, nor revilers, nor swindlers will inherit the kingdom of God."
2. ***Proverbs 15:27*** – "Whoever is greedy for unjust gain troubles his own household, but he who hates bribes will live."
3. ***Psalm 37:21*** – "The wicked borrows and does not pay back, but the righteous is generous and gives."
4. ***Titus 1:7*** – "For an overseer (Elder of the church), as God's steward, must be above reproach. He must not be arrogant or quick-tempered or a drunkard or violent or greedy for gain."
5. ***Matthew 23:25*** – "Woe to you, scribes and Pharisees, hypocrites! For you clean the outside of the cup and the plate, but inside are full of greed and self-indulgence."
6. ***2 Peter 2:2-3*** – "And many will follow their (false prophets and teachers) sensuality, and because of them the way of truth will be blasphemed. And in their greed, they will exploit you with false words. Their condemnation from long ago is not idle, and their destruction will not sleep."

CHAPTER TWO:
THE VIRTUE OF CHASTITY

What is the Virtue of Chastity?

Controlling thoughts, words and actions
Honoring your body as Jehovah God's temple
Abstinence from pre-marital sex
Sexual purity
Tolerance in judging others.
Impacting the lives of others in a positive way
Treating others with respect
Yielding to God's plan and purpose for your life

Chastity refers to the state or practice of refraining from extramarital sexual intercourse. In 1 Corinthians 10:8, Jehovah God warns us about the consequences of not being chaste, "Nor let us act immorally, as some of them did, and twenty-three thousand fell in one day." In the Book of Exodus 20:40, sexual chastity is recommended, and a serious warning is placed on the vice of adultery, "Do not commit adultery." Our bodies as a temple of Jehovah God must be kept clean and chaste. 1 Corinthians 6:18-20 warns "Flee immorality. Every other sin that a man commits is outside the body, but the immoral man sins against his own body. Or do you not know that your body is a temple of the Holy Spirit who is in you, whom you have from God, and that you are not your own? For you have been bought with a price: therefore, glorify God in your body."

It is the will of Jehovah God that we refrain from sexual immorality for our Sanctification (1 Thessalonians 4:3)

Math for the Grateful Soul: Gratitude + Chastity = Gratichastitude

Gratichastitude refers to the readiness to practice purity or abstinence as a show of appreciation or gratitude to Jehovah God. Believers must therefore look up to Jehovah God for Godly Standards and not in the world.

Gratefulness
Recognition
Appreciation
Thankfulness
Indebtedness
Compassion
Honor
Altruism
Sexual purity
Treating others with respect
Impact
Tolerance
Understanding
Devotedness
Enthusiasm

The Benefits of Chastity Before Marriage

The readiness to practice purity or abstinence from sexual intercourse before marriage as a show of appreciation or gratitude to Jehovah God comes with amazing health benefits. Though Nearly every religion teaches the principle of chastity before marriage, fewer and fewer people are observing it, and today's culture is not helping either. However, those who show Jehovah God gratitude by abstaining from sexual intercourse before marriage are highly rewarded. True manhood should therefore not seek to compromise a woman's purity but should stand to heroically protect it. Abstinence before marriage may lower the incidents of psychological damage from practicing intimacy without commitment, freedom from sexually transmitted diseases (STDs) and unwanted pregnancies, and an increase in marital stability and satisfaction.

What the New International Version of the Holy Bible Says about Chastity

1. ***Colossians 3:5*** – Put to death, therefore, whatever belongs to your earthly nature: sexual immorality, impurity, lust, evil desires and greed, which is idolatry.
2. ***1 Corinthians 7:1-*** Now for the matters you wrote about: "It is good for a man not to have sexual relations with a woman."
3. ***1 Corinthians 6:18*** – Flee from sexual immorality. All other sins a person commits are outside the

body, but whoever sins sexually, sins against their own body.

4. ***1 Corinthians 7:7-9*** –I wish that all of you were as I am. But each of you has your own gift from God; one has this gift, another has that. Now to the unmarried and the widows I say: It is good for them to stay unmarried, as I do. But if they cannot control themselves, they should marry, for it is better to marry than to burn with passion.

5. ***1 Corinthians 6:13*** - You say, "Food for the stomach and the stomach for food, and God will destroy them both." The body, however, is not meant for sexual immorality but for the LORD, and the LORD for the body.

6. ***Ephesians 5:3*** –But among you there must not be even a hint of sexual immorality, or of any kind of impurity, or of greed, because these are improper for God's holy people.

7. ***Exodus 20:14-*** You shall not commit adultery.

8. ***Galatians 5:19*** - The acts of the flesh are obvious: sexual immorality, impurity and debauchery.

9. ***Hebrews 13:4*** – Marriage should be honored by all, and the marriage bed kept pure, for God will judge the adulterer and all the sexually immoral.

10. ***Leviticus 20:13-*** If a man has sexual relations with a man as one does with a woman, both have done what is detestable. They are to be put to death; their blood will be on their own heads.

11. *Mathew 5* :8- Blessed are the pure in heart: for they shall see God
12. *Matthew 5:28* – But I tell you that anyone who looks at a woman lustfully has already committed adultery with her in his heart.
13. *Romans 13:13* –Let us behave decently, as in the daytime, not in carousing and drunkenness, not in sexual immorality and debauchery, not in dissension and jealousy.
14. *1 Thessalonians 4:3-* It is God's will that you should be sanctified: that you should avoid sexual immorality.
15. *1 Thessalonians 4:7* –For God did not call us to be impure, but to live a holy life.

GREAT QUOTES ON CHASTITY

- "Chastity is the cement of civilization and progress. Without it there is no stability in society, and without it one cannot attain the science of life." ~ *Mary Eddy*
- "The moral code of Heaven for both men and women is complete chastity before marriage and full fidelity after marriage." ~*Ezra Taft Benson*
- "Modesty and chastity are important values for us, and we are not giving them up." ~*Antonio Sciortino*
- "When you decide firmly to lead a clean life, chastity will not be a burden on you; it will be a crown of triumph." ~ *St. Josemaria Escriva*

- "A man defines his standing at the court of chastity by his views of women." ~*Amos Bronson Alcott*
- "Chastity is more a state of mind than of anatomy." ~*Edward Abbey*
- "The essence of chastity is not the suppression of lust, but total orientation of one's life towards a goal." ~*Dietrich Bonhoeffer*
- "Chastity is a difficult long-term matter; one must wait patiently for it to bear fruit, for the happiness of loving kindness which it must bring. But at the same time, chastity is the sure way to happiness." ~*John Paul 11*
- "Chastity is one of the greatest disciplines without which the mind cannot attain requisite firmness." ~*M.K. Gandhi*

Math for the Ungrateful Soul: Chastity - Gratitude = lust

Lust is described as a strong inappropriate sexual desire. Whenever we fail to refrain from extramarital sexual intercourse, we become lustful in the eyes of Jehovah God and we cultivate ungrateful souls. Our maker Jehovah God does not only require us to abstain from extramarital sexual intercourse but appreciates it if we can avoid yielding into temptation and honoring our bodies as his temple. An attitude of gratitude makes it easier to control thoughts, words actions and surrendering to God's plan and purpose for one's life.

"Marriage doesn't cure lust, if it did adultery wouldn't exist. Self-control is still a requirement. Lust doesn't care if you are married or single. You may be Solomon in wisdom or David in praise or Abraham in faith or Joshua in war but if you are not Joseph in discipline, you will end up like Samson in destruction..." - ***Nelson Mandela***

What the New International Version of the Holy Bible Says about lust

1. ***Colossians 3:5***- "Put to death, therefore, whatever belongs to your earthly nature: sexual immorality, impurity, **lust**, evil desires and greed, which is idolatry."

2. ***1 Corinthians 6:13***- "You say, Food for the stomach and the stomach for food, and God will destroy them both. The body, however, is not meant for sexual immorality but for the LORD, and the LORD for the body."

3. ***2 Corinthians 6:18***- "And, I will be a Father to you, and you will be my sons and daughters, says the LORD Almighty."

4. ***Ephesians 5:3***- "But among you there must not be even a hint of sexual immorality, or of any kind of impurity, or of greed, because these are improper for God's holy people."

5. ***Ephesians 5:5*** – "For of this you can be sure: No immoral, impure or greedy person-such a person is an idolater-has any inheritance in the kingdom of Christ and of God."

6. *Hebrews 13:4*- "Marriage should be honored by all, and the marriage bed kept pure, for God will judge the adulterer and all the sexually immoral."

7. *1 John 2:16*- "For everything in the world—the lust of the flesh, the lust of the eyes, and the pride of life—comes not from the Father but from the world."

8. *Mathew 5:28*- "But I tell you that anyone who looks at a woman lustfully has already committed adultery with her in his heart."

9. **1 Thessalonians 4:3-5**- "It is God's will that you should be sanctified: that you should avoid sexual immorality; that each of you should learn to control your own body in a way that is holy and honorable, not in passionate lust like the pagans, who do not know God;"

10. **Proverbs 6:32**- "But a man who commits adultery has no sense; whoever does so destroy himself."

CHAPTER THREE: THE VIRTUE OF DILIGENCE

What is the Virtue of Diligence?

Dedication
Industriousness
Lifelong learning
Indefatigability
God-fearing
Endeavor
Niceness
Conscientiousness
Effort

Diligence is the constant effort to accomplish what is undertaken; exertion of body or mind without unnecessary delay or sloth; due attention; industry; assiduity. Diligence is the philosophers stone that turns everything to gold. Diligence, in Christianity, is the effort to do one's part, while keeping faith and reliance in God. It means to be **prudent** (plan, forecast, project, anticipate, provision)**, be wise (learn from experience), deeply ponder,** and to do this consistently (every time, all the time).

"Difficulties break some men but make others. No axe is sharp enough to cut the soul of a sinner who keeps on trying, one armed with the hope that he will rise even in the end." ~*Nelson Mandela*

What the New International Version of the Holy Bible Says About Diligence

1. ***Deuteronomy 4:29-*** "But if from there you seek the LORD your God, you will find him if you seek him with all your heart and with all your soul."
2. ***Deuteronomy 6:17-*** "Be sure to keep the commands of the LORD your God and the stipulations and decrees he has given you."
3. ***2 Peter 1:5*** - For this very reason, make every effort to add to your faith goodness; and to goodness, knowledge;
4. ***Proverbs 4:23*** - Above all else, guard your heart, for everything you do flows from it.
5. ***Romans 12:11-*** Never be lacking in zeal, but keep your spiritual fervor, serving the LORD.
6. ***2 Timothy 2:15-*** Do your best to present yourself to God as one approved, a worker who does not need to be ashamed and who correctly handles the word of truth.
7. ***Hebrews 6:11-*** We want each of you to show this same diligence to the very end, so that what you hope for may be fully realized.

8. ***Hebrews 11:6-*** And without faith it is impossible to please God, because anyone who comes to him must believe that he exists and that he rewards those who earnestly seek him.

9. ***Ecclesiastes 9:10-*** Whatever your hand finds to do, do it with all your might, for in the realm of the dead, where you are going, there is neither working nor planning nor knowledge nor wisdom.

10. ***Proverbs 8:17-*** *I love those who love me, and those who seek me find me.*

11. ***Proverbs 10:4-*** Lazy hands make for poverty, but diligent hands bring wealth.

12. ***Proverbs 11:27-*** Whoever seeks good finds favor, but evil comes to one who searches for it.

13. ***Proverbs 12:24-*** Diligent hands will rule, but laziness ends in forced labor.

14. ***Proverbs 12:27-*** The lazy do not roast any game, but the diligent feed on the riches of the hunt.

15. ***Proverbs 13:4-*** A sluggard's appetite is never filled, but the desires of the diligent are fully satisfied.

16. ***Proverbs 16:3-*** Commit to the LORD whatever you do, and he will establish your plans.

17. ***Proverbs 21:5-*** The plans of the diligent lead to profit as surely as haste leads to poverty.

18. ***Joshua 1:8-*** Keep this Book of the Law always on your lips; meditate on its day and night, so that you

may be careful to do everything written in it. Then you will be prosperous and successful.

19. ***Colossians 3:23-*** Whatever you do, work at it with all your heart, as working for the Lord, not for human masters, since you know that you will receive an inheritance from the Lord as a reward. It is the Lord Christ you are serving.

20. ***Galatians 6:9-*** Let us not become weary in doing good, for at the proper time we will reap a harvest if we do not give up.

What Some Great Minds Say About Diligence

- "Let's be diligent in giving, careful in our living, and faithful in our praying." *- **Jack Hyles***

- "I am afraid that the schools will prove the very gates of hell, unless they diligently labor in explaining the Holy Scriptures and engraving them in the heart of the youth." *- **Martin Luther***

- "Are you still diligently living for God and serving Him, even in these last days? Now is not the time to ease up, but to charge forward and continue living for the Lord."*- **Paul Chappell***

- "Dignity does not float down from heaven it cannot be purchased nor manufactured. It is a reward reserved for those who labor with diligence"*- **Bill Hybels***

- "Diligence overcomes difficulties, sloth makes them." - ***Benjamin Franklin***
- "The expectations of life depend upon diligence; the mechanic that would perfect his work must first sharpen his tools."- **Confucius**
- "Diligence is the mother of good fortune". - ***Benjamin Disraeli***
- "That which ordinary men are fit for, I am qualified in and the best of me is diligence." **William Shakespeare**
- "Be a lamp unto yourself. Work out your liberation with diligence."- ***Buddha***
- "Chaos is inherent in all compounded things. Strive on with diligence."- ***Buddha***
- "I have been very fortunate in worldly matters many men have worked much harder, and not succeeded half so well but I never could have done what I have done, without the habits of punctuality, order, and diligence, without the determination to concentrate myself on one object at a time, no matter how quickly its successor should come upon its heels, which I then formed." ~ ***Charles Dickens***

Math for the Grateful Soul: Gratitude + Diligence = Gratidiligenitude

Gratidiligenitude refers to the exercise of persistence, effort and ethics as a show of appreciation to Jehovah God.

Gratefulness
Recognition
Appreciation
Thankfulness
Indebtedness
Dedication
Industriousness
Lifelong learning
Indefatigability
God-fearing
Endeavor
Niceness
Intuition
Teachability
Understanding
Devotedness
Effort

Math for the Ungrateful Soul: Diligence - Gratitude = Sloth

Sloth or laziness is reluctance to work or try; laziness. Sloth or Laziness is a disinclination to activity or exertion despite having the ability to act or exert oneself.

Laziness is condemned throughout the Holy Bible and in many doctrines of good living. Jehovah God created man in his own image and in doing so, equipped man with all it takes to work for six out of the seven days he created and to rest for one day. He discouraged sloth from the very beginning of humanity and that position has never changed. If you do your best in every good thing or assignment God has given you, he will surely fulfil his promise of doing the rest for you. In the Book of Mathew, it is written "But seek first his kingdom and his righteousness, and all these things will be given to you as well." (***Mathew 6:33***). Seeking the Kingdom of God involves seeking the knowledge, understanding and the wisdom about God's kingdom, this involves hard work. A Sloth attitude will not enable you seek God's Kingdom, and all the other things that need hard work will surely not be added unto you.

What the New International Version of the Bible Says About Sloth

1. ***Proverbs 6:6-9*** – "Go to the ant, you sluggard; consider its ways and be wise! It has no commander, no overseer or ruler, yet it stores it provisions in summer and gathers its food at harvest. How long will you lie there, you sluggard? When will you get up from your sleep?"
2. ***Proverbs 10:26-27-*** "As vinegar to the teeth and smoke to the eyes, so are sluggards to those who send them. The fear of the LORD adds length to life, but the years of the wicked are cut short."
3. ***Proverbs 15:19-*** "The way of the sluggard is blocked with thorns, but the path of the upright is a highway."
4. ***Proverbs 18 :9*** – "One who is slack in his work is brother to one who destroys."

5. ***Proverbs 19:15*** - "Laziness brings on deep sleep, and the shiftless go hungry."
6. **Proverbs 20:4** - Sluggards do not plow in season; so, at harvest time they look but find nothing.
7. ***Proverbs 20:**13* – "Do not love sleep or you will grow poor; stay awake and you will have food to spare."
8. ***Proberbs21:25-26*** – "The craving of a sluggard will be the death of him, because his hands refuse to work. All day long he craves for more, but the righteous give without sparing."
9. ***Proverbs 26:14-16*** – "As a door turns on its hinges, so a sluggard turns on his bed. A sluggard buries his hand in the dish; he is too lazy to bring it back to his mouth. A sluggard is wiser in his own eyes than seven people who answer discreetly."
10. ***Proverbs 31:13*** – "A godly woman is not lazy "She selects wool and flax and works with eager hands."

CHAPTER FOUR:
THE VIRTUE OF FAITH

What is the Virtue of Faith?
Filled with the fullness of God
Aspiration as expressed in the quest for God
Infinite love of God
Trust in God
Hope in God

What is Faith? "Now faith is confidence in what we hope for and assurance about what we do not see. This is what the ancients were commended for. By faith we understand that the universe was formed at God's command, so that what is seen was not made out of what was visible." Faith is a crucial link in every believer's life because when failure keeps you humble, when success keeps you glowing, only FAITH and Determination can keep you going.

Faith is a crucial ingredient in every believer's life and no book in the holy Bible defines faith or celebrates the champions of faith like the book of Hebrews. For some reason or reasons known to Jehovah God and maybe Christ and the holy spirit, the author of the book of Hebrews remains a mystery. Knowing who Jehovah God is, how he created man and woman in his own very image, I dare to think that the author of the book of Hebrews was a wise woman.

Her identity has been kept a secret all these years because Jehovah God wants believers to focus more on the message of faith and not on the messenger. May Jehovah God be praised.

What the New International Version of the Holy Bible Says About Faith

1. **Mathew 17:20** - He replied, "Because you have so little faith. Truly I tell you, if you have faith as small as a mustard seed, you can say to this mountain, 'Move from here to there,' and it will move. Nothing will be impossible for you."

2. **Romans 10:17** - "Consequently, faith comes from hearing the message, and the message is heard through the word about Christ."

3. **Mathew 21:22** - "If you believe, you will receive whatever you ask for in prayer."

4. **Hebrew 11:6** - "And without faith it is impossible to please God, because anyone who comes to him must believe that he exists and that he rewards those who earnestly seek him."

5. **Ephesians 2:8-9** – "For it is by grace you have been saved, through faith-and this is not from yourselves, it is the gift of God- not by works, so that no one can boast."

6. **Luke 1:37** – "For no word from God will ever fail."

7. **Proverbs 3:5-6** - Trust in the LORD with all your heart and lean not on your own understanding; in all your ways submit to him, and he will make your paths straight.
8. **I Corinthians 2:5** - So that your faith might not rest on human wisdom, but on God's power.
9. **2 Corinthians 5:7**- For we live by faith, not by sight.
10. **John 3:16** - For God so loved the world that he gave his one and only Son, that whoever believes in him shall not perish but have eternal life.

Some Luminary Members of the Hebrew Hall of Faith:

- **Enoch:** By faith Enoch was taken from this life, so that he did not experience death: "He could not be found, because God had taken him away." For before he was taken, he was commended as one who pleased God. And without faith it is impossible to please God, because anyone who comes to him must believe that he exists and that he rewards those who earnestly seek him (Hebrew 11:5-6, NIV).

- **Noah:** By faith Noah, when warned about things not yet seen, in holy fear built an ark to save his family. By his faith he condemned the world and became heir of the righteousness that is in keeping with faith. (Hebrews *11:7* - NIV).

▲ **Abraham:** By faith Abraham, when called to go to a place he would later receive as his inheritance, obeyed and went, even though he did not know where he was going. By faith he made his home in the promised land like a stranger in a foreign country; he lived in tents, as did Isaac and Jacob, who were heirs with him of the same promise. For he was looking forward to the city with foundations, whose architect and builder is God ***(Hebrews 11:8-10, NIV)***.

And so, from this one man, and he as good as dead, came descendants as numerous as the stars in the sky and as countless as the sand on the seashore. All these people were still living by faith when they died. They did not receive the things promised; they only saw them and welcomed them from a distance, admitting that they were foreigners and strangers on earth. People who say such things show that they are looking for a country of their own. If they had been thinking of the country they had left, they would have had opportunity to return. Instead, they were longing for a better country-a heavenly one. Therefore, God is not ashamed to be called their God, for he has prepared a city for them. By faith Abraham, when God tested him, offered Isaac as a sacrifice. He who had embraced the promises was about to sacrifice his one and only son, even though God had said to him, "It is through Isaac that your offspring will be reckoned." Abraham reasoned that God could even raise the dead, and so in a manner of speaking he did receive Isaac back from death (***Hebrews 11:12-19, NIV***).

- **Sarah:** And by faith even Sarah, who was past childbearing age, was enabled to bear children because she considered him faithful who had made the promise (*Hebrews 11:11, NIV*).

- **Isaac, Jacob & Joseph:** By faith Isaac blessed Jacob and Esau regarding their future. By faith Jacob, when he was dying, blessed each of Joseph's sons, and worshiped as he leaned on the top of his staff. By faith Joseph, when his end was near, spoke about the exodus of the Israelites from Egypt and gave instructions concerning the burial of his bones (*Hebrews 11:20-22*, **NIV**).

- **Moses, Amram, & Jochebed**: By faith Moses' parents hid him for three months after he was born, because they saw he was no ordinary child, and they were not afraid of the king's edict. By faith Moses, when he had grown up, refused to be known as the son of Pharaoh's daughter. He chose to be mistreated along with the people of God rather than to enjoy the fleeting pleasures of sin. He regarded disgrace for the sake of Christ as of greater value than the treasures of Egypt, because he was looking ahead to his reward. By faith he left Egypt, not fearing the king's anger; he persevered because he saw him who is invisible. By faith he kept the Passover and the application of blood, so that the destroyer of the firstborn would not touch the firstborn of Israel. By faith the people passed through the Red Sea as on dry land; but when the Egyptians tried to do so, they were drowned (**Hebrews 11:23-29, NIV**).

▲ **Joshua & Rehab:** By faith the walls of Jericho fell, after the army had marched around them for seven days. ³¹By faith the prostitute Rahab, because she welcomed the spies, was not killed with those who were disobedient *(Hebrews 11:30-31,* **NIV**).

Types of Faith

1. **Natural faith, everyone has natural faith which gives confidence** *(Mathew 16:1-3)*

   The Pharisees and Sadducees came to Jesus and tested him by asking him to show them a sign from heaven. He replied, "When evening comes, you say, 'It will be fair weather, for the sky is red,' and in the morning, 'Today it will be stormy, for the sky is red and overcast.' You know how to interpret the appearance of the sky, but you cannot interpret the signs of the times. (Mathew 16:1-3, NIV).

2. **Saving faith leads us to salvation** *(Romans 10:8-13)*

   But what does it say? "The word is near you; it is in your mouth and in your heart," that is, the message concerning faith that we proclaim: If you declare with your mouth, "Jesus is LORD," and believe in your heart that God raised him from the dead, you will be saved. For it is with your heart that you believe and are justified, and it is with your mouth that you profess your faith and are saved. As Scripture says,

"Anyone who believes in him will never be put to shame." For there is no difference between Jew and Gentile-the same LORD is LORD of all and richly blesses all who call on him, for, "Everyone who calls on the name of the LORD will be saved." (***Romans 10:8-13, NIV***).

3. **Active faith enables us to experience God's power** (*Luke 7:45-50*)

    You did not give me a kiss, but this woman, from the time I entered, has not stopped kissing my feet. You did not put oil on my head, but she has poured perfume on my feet. Therefore, I tell you, her many sins have been forgiven-as her great love has shown. But whoever has been forgiven little loves little." Then Jesus said to her, "Your sins are forgiven." The other guests began to say among themselves, "Who is this who even forgives sins?" Jesus said to the woman, "Your faith has saved you; go in peace." (***Luke 7:45-50, NIV***).

4. **Overcoming faith empowers us to live victoriously** (*1 John 4-5*)

    "In him was life, and that life was the light of all mankind. The light shines in the darkness, and the darkness has not overcome it."

Steps to Grow Your Faith

1. Know and accept Christ as your Lord and Savior

2. Stand on your own faith by believing God for yourself
3. Step up to serve Christ by serving others
4. Share Christ by sharing your faith

What Some Great Minds Say About Faith in God

1. "I believe in Christianity as I believe that the sun has risen not only because I see it, but because by it I see everything else." ~ *C.S. Lewis*
2. "Never be afraid to trust an unknown future to a known God." ~ *Corrie ten Boom*
3. "All I have seen teaches me to trust the Creator for all I have not seen." ~ *Ralph Waldo Emerson*
4. The greatest legacy one can pass on to one's children and grandchildren is not money or other material things accumulated in one's life, but rather a legacy of character and faith ~ *Billy Graham*
5. Every tomorrow has two handles. We can take hold of it with the handle of anxiety or the handle of faith ~ *Henry Ward Beecher*
6. Faith is taking the first step even when you don't see the whole staircase ~ *Martin Luther King Jr.*
7. The situations that will stretch your faith most will be those times when life falls apart and God is nowhere to be found. This happened to Job ~ *Rick Warren*

8. Seeds of faith are always within us; sometimes it takes a crisis to nourish and encourage their growth. ~ ***Myles Munroe***

9. Faith is not only daring to believe, it is also daring to act. When I believe in myself as a son of God, I attribute to all men the same quality. This goes for men of every class, creed and color. The proof that I believe this way will be measured by the way I act towards others ~ ***Wilfred Peterson***

10. Every day you need to get a full dose of the Word and Meditate on scripture, and if you discipline yourself and remain consistent, your faith will grow and mature, and remember that God, the Word, and your faith, is a recipe for success ~ ***Stephanie Williams***

11. Faith is not the power of positive thinking; it is believing in God and trusting that His will is always best even when you cannot understand why ~ ***Shari Howerton***

12. The whole being of any Christian is faith and love. Faith brings the person to God, love brings the person to people. ~ ***Martin Luther***

Math for the Grateful Soul: Gratitude + Faith = Gratifaithitude

Gratifaithitude refers to the ability to be thankful for the things that we hope for, the evidence of things not yet seen.

Gratefulness
Recognition
Appreciation
Teachability
Filled with the fullness of God
Aspiration as expressed in the quest for God
Infinite love of God
Trust in God
Hope in God
Indebtedness, feeling of owing gratitude for a service or favor
Thankfulness, expressing gratitude to God
Understanding, having insight or good judgement
Devotedness, a state of being faithful
Enthusiasm, intense and eager enjoyment, interest, or approval

Math for the Ungrateful Soul: Faith - Gratitude = Fear.

Fear is the feeling of the likelihood of something unwelcome happening. As brilliantly stated by the luminary late Nelson Mandela, courage is not the absence of fear, but the triumph over it and the brave man is not he who does not feel afraid, but he who conquers that fear. "Let the first act of every morning be to make the following resolve for the day: I shall not fear anyone on Earth, I shall fear only God."- *Mahatma Ghandi*

What the New International Version of the Bible Says About Fear:

1. ***Isaiah 41:10*** - So do not fear, for I am with you; do not be dismayed, for I am your God. I will strengthen you and help you; I will uphold you with my righteous right hand.

2. ***2 Timothy 1:7*** – For the Spirit God gave us does not make us timid, but gives us power, love and self-discipline.

3. ***1 John 4:18*** – There is no fear in love. But perfect love drives out fear, because fear has to do with punishment. The one who fears is not made perfect in love.

4. ***Psalms 23:1-6*** - The LORD is my shepherd, I lack nothing. He makes me lie down in green pastures, he leads me beside quiet waters, he refreshes my soul. He guides me along the right paths for his name's sake. Even though I walk through the darkest valley, I will fear no evil, for you are with me; your rod and your staff, they comfort me. You prepare a table before me in the presence of my enemies. You anoint my head with oil; my cup overflows. Surely your goodness and love will follow me all the days of my life, and I will dwell in the house of the LORD forever.

5. ***Psalms 34:4*** – "I sought the LORD, and he answered me; he delivered me from all my fears."

6. ***Proverbs 29:25*** - "Fear of man will prove to be a snare, but whoever trusts in the LORD is kept safe."

7. ***Philippians 4:6*** - "Do not be anxious about anything, but in every situation, by prayer and petition, with thanksgiving, present your requests to God."

8. ***Psalms 56:3-4*** - "When I am afraid, I put my trust in you. ⁴In God, whose word I praise- in God I trust and am not afraid. What can mere mortals do to me?"

9. ***Romans 8:15*** - "The Spirit you received does not make you slaves, so that you live in fear again; rather, the Spirit you received brought about your adoption to sonship. And by him we cry, "Abba, Father."

10. ***Romans 8:38-39*** - "For I am convinced that neither death nor life, neither angels nor demons, neither the present nor the future, nor any powers, neither height nor depth, nor anything else in all creation, will be able to separate us from the love of God that is in Christ Jesus our LORD."

11. ***Isaiah 43:1-3*** - "But now, this is what the LORD says- he who created you, Jacob, he who formed you, Israel: "Do not fear, for I have redeemed you; I have summoned you by name; you are mine. When you pass through the waters, I will be with you; and when you pass through the rivers, they will not sweep over you. When you walk through the fire, you will not be burned; the flames will not set you ablaze. For I am the LORD your God, the Holy One of Israel, your

Savior; I give Egypt for your ransom, Cush and Seba in your stead."

12. **Proverbs 19:23** – "The fear of the LORD leads to life; then one rests content, untouched by trouble."

What Nelson Mandela Says About Fear

1. I learned that courage was not the absence of fear, but the triumph over it. The brave man is not he who does not feel afraid, but he who conquers that fear.
2. A good head and a good heart are always a formidable combination
3. As we are liberated from our own fear, our presence automatically liberates others.
4. Forgiveness liberates the soul. It removes fear. That is why it is such a powerful weapon.
5. Let your choices reflect your hopes and not your fears
6. Our deepest fear is not that we are inadequate. Our deepest fear is that we are powerful beyond measure.
7. Courageous people do not fear forgiving, for the sake of peace

CHAPTER FIVE: THE VIRTUE OF FORTITUDE

What is the Virtue of Fortitude?

Firmness of purpose
Open-mindedness towards others
Resilience
Trustworthiness
Intrepid spirit
Treating others with respect
Undaunting spirit
Determination
Endurance

Fortitude is the strength of character that enables a person to endure pain or adversity with courage. Although the word fortitude is rarely used in the most popular versions of the Bible, the concept is addressed often.

What the New International Version of the Holy Bible Says About Fortitude:

1. ***John 15:18-19*** – "If the world hates you, keep in mind that it hated me first. If you belonged to the world, it would love you as its own. As it is, you do

not belong to the world, but I have chosen you out of the world. That is why the world hates you."

2. ***Isaiah 53:7*** – "He was oppressed and afflicted, yet he did not open his mouth; he was led like a lamb to the slaughter, and as a sheep before its shearers is silent, so he did not open his mouth."

3. ***Genesis 3:21*** – "The LORD God made garments of skin for Adam and his wife and clothed them."

4. ***1 John 5:19*** – "We know that we are children of God, and that the whole world is under the control of the evil one."

5. ***Romans 8:28*** – "And we know that in all things God works for the good of those who love him, who have been called according to his purpose."

What Some Great Minds Say About Fortitude

- ***Saint Augustine:*** "Fortitude is the disposition of soul which enables us to despise all inconveniences and the loss of things not in our power."

- ***Muhammad Ali:*** "He who is not courageous enough to take risks will accomplish nothing in life."

- ***John Locke***: "Fortitude is the guard and support of the other virtues."

- ***Winston Churchill***: "Courage is what it takes to stand up and speak; courage is also what it takes to sit down and listen."

- *Confucius*: "To be fond of learning is near to wisdom; to practice with vigor is near to benevolence; and to be conscious of shame is near to fortitude."
- *Titus Maccius Plautus*: "Fortitude is a great help in distress."
- *Erich Fromm:* "Fortitude is the capacity to say no when the world wants to hear yes."
- *François de La Rochefoucauld*: "All of us have sufficient fortitude to bear the misfortunes of others."
- *John F. Kennedy*: "Efforts and courage are not enough without purpose and direction."

Math for the Grateful Soul: Gratitude + Fortitude = Gratifortitude

Gratifortitude refers to a show of patience, perseverance and courage in pain or adversity as a sign of gratitude to Jehovah, God.

Gratefulness
Recognition
Appreciation
Teachability
Intuition
Firmness of purpose
Open-mindedness towards others
Resilience
Trustworthiness
Intrepid spirit

Treating others with respect
Undaunting spirit
Determination
Endurance

Math for the Ungrateful Soul: Fortitude – Gratitude = Faintheartedness

Faintheartedness refers to the lack of courage, timid. The word of God as written and translated in the various versions of the Holy Bible celebrates the courageous bible heroes such as David (I Samuel 17:41-52), Daniel (Daniel 6:20-22), Shadrach, Meshach, Abednego (Daniel 3:16-28) and many more. This same Holy Bible does not hesitate to warn the fainthearted in many of the books of the Holy Bible.

What the New International Version of the Holy Bible Says About Faintheartedness

1. ***2 Corinthians 4:16*** - Therefore we do not lose heart. Though outwardly we are wasting away, yet inwardly we are being renewed day by day.
2. ***1 Thessalonians 5:15*** - Make sure that nobody pays back wrong for wrong, but always strive to do what is good for each other and for everyone else.
3. ***Psalm 73:26*** - My flesh and my heart may fail, but God is the strength of my heart and my portion forever.
4. ***Proverbs 28:1*** – The wicked flee though no one pursues, but the righteous are as bold as a lion.

5. ***Revelations 21:8*** – But the cowardly, the unbelieving, the vile, the murderers, the sexually immoral, those who practice magic arts, the idolaters and all liars—they will be consigned to the fiery lake of burning sulfur. This is the second death.

6. ***Luke 22:54–62*** – Then seizing him, they led him away and took him into the house of the high priest. Peter followed at a distance. And when some there had kindled a fire in the middle of the courtyard and had sat down together, Peter sat down with them. A servant girl saw him seated there in the firelight. She looked closely at him and said, "This man was with him."

   But he denied it. "Woman, I don't know him," he said. A little later someone else saw him and said, "You also are one of them." "Man, I am not!" Peter replied.

   About an hour later another asserted, "Certainly this fellow was with him, for he is a Galilean." Peter replied, "Man, I don't know what you're talking about!" Just as he was speaking, the rooster crowed. The Lord turned and looked straight at Peter. Then Peter remembered the word the Lord had spoken to him: "Before the rooster crows today, you will disown me three times." And he went outside and wept bitterly.

7. ***Joshua 10*** :25 - Joshua said to them, "Do not be afraid; do not be discouraged. Be strong and courageous. This is what the LORD will do to all the enemies you are going to fight."

8. ***Isiah 41***:8-10 - "But you, Israel, my servant, Jacob, whom I have chosen, you descendants of Abraham

my friend, I took you from the ends of the earth, from its farthest corners I called you I said, 'You are my servant'; I have chosen you and have not rejected you. So do not fear, for I am with you; do not be dismayed, for I am your God I will strengthen you and help you; I will uphold you with my righteous right hand.

What Some Great Minds Say About Faintheartedness

- Far better it is to dare mighty things, to win glorious triumphs, even though checkered by failure, Than to take rank with those poor spirits who neither enjoy much nor suffer much, because they live in the gray twilight that knows neither victory nor defeat ~ ***Theodore Roosevelt***

- Better to jump in the water and learn to swim than stand on the shore wondering ~ ***Alexander Pope***

- If we spend our days trying to avoid the landmines of stepping out of God's will, then will be afraid to take any risks for his kingdom. But when you know there is a net of grace, when you know that God will catch you and set you back on his path when you fall, then you'll feel the freedom to pursue the adventure that kingdom living is all about. ~ ***Will Davis Jr.***

- When you believe in your dream and your vision, then it begins to attract its own resources. No one was born to be a failure. ~ ***Myles Munroe***

CHAPTER SIX:
THE VIRTUE OF HUMILITY

What is the Virtue of Humility?

Humbleness
Understanding
Meekness
Infinite love of God
Liberality
Impacting the lives of others in a positive way
Tolerance
Yielding to God's plan and purpose for your life

Humility is the quality of being humble. Humility comes from the Latin word humilis, which literally means low. Humility is the fear of the LORD; its wages are riches and honor and life (***Proverbs 22:4***). In the Bible, humility or humbleness is a quality of being courteously respectful of others. It is the opposite of aggressiveness, arrogance, boastfulness, and vanity. Godly humility is being comfortable with who you are in the Lord and therefore putting others first.

Godly humility is the act of being comfortable with who you are in Christ as the son of Jehovah God, and seeking to build others up, not yourself. It is gratefully walking in God's grace, love, and forgiveness. "Do nothing out of selfish ambition or vain conceit, but in humility consider others better than yourselves." *(Philippians 2:3)*. Even though Jesus Christ was the Son of God who could demand some bragging rights, he became an excellent example of humility in action. Although he was the son of God in human flesh, he was gentle and humble–and he was strong. The Book of Mathew paints a clear picture of his words that always matched his actions. "Come to me, all you who are weary and burdened, and I will give you rest. Take my yoke upon you and learn from me, for I am gentle and humble in heart, and you will find rest for your souls. For my yoke is easy and my burden is light." *(Mathew 11:28-30)*

What the New International Version of the Holy Bible Says About Humility

1. ***Genesis 18:22*** - The men turned away and went toward Sodom, but Abraham remained standing before the LORD.
2. ***Genesis 41:16*** - I cannot do it, Joseph replied to Pharaoh, "but God will give Pharaoh the answer he desires."
3. ***2 Corinthians 10:1*** - By the humility and gentleness of Christ, I appeal to you—I, Paul, who am "timid" when face to face with you, but "bold" toward you when away!
4. ***Exodus 3:11*** - But Moses said to God, "Who am I that I should go to Pharaoh and bring the Israelites out of Egypt?"

5. ***Psalm 113:4-9*** - The LORD is exalted over all the nations, his glory above the heavens. Who is like the LORD our God, the One who sits enthroned on high, who stoops down to look on the heavens and the earth? He raises the poor from the dust and lifts the needy from the ash heap; he seats them with princes, with the princes of his people. He settles the childless woman in her home as a happy mother of children. Praise the LORD.

6. ***Psalm 138:6-7*** - Though the LORD is exalted, he looks kindly on the lowly; though lofty, he sees them from afar. Though I walk in the midst of trouble, you preserve my life. You stretch out your hand against the anger of my foes; with your right hand you save me.

7. ***Mathew 11:28-29*** - "Come to me, all you who are weary and burdened, and I will give you rest. Take my yoke upon you and learn from me, for I am gentle and humble in heart, and you will find rest for your souls

8. ***Philippians 2:3-11*** - Do nothing out of selfish ambition or vain conceit. Rather, in humility value others above yourselves, not looking to your own interests but each of you to the interests of the others. In your relationships with one another, have the same mindset as Christ Jesus: Who, being in very nature God, did not consider equality with God something to be used to his own advantage; rather, he made himself nothing by taking the very nature of a servant, being made in human likeness. And being found in

appearance as a man, he humbled himself by becoming obedient to death- even death on a cross! Therefore, God exalted him to the highest place and gave him the name that is above every name, that at the name of Jesus every knee should bow, in heaven and on earth and under the earth, and every tongue acknowledge that Jesus Christ is LORD, to the glory of God the Father.

9. *Philippians 2:5-8* - In your relationships with one another, have the same mindset as Christ Jesus: Who, being in very nature God, did not consider equality with God something to be used to his own advantage; rather, he made himself nothing by taking the very nature of a servant, being made in human likeness.

10. *James 4:6* - But he gives us more grace. That is why Scripture says: "God opposes the proud but shows favor to the humble."

11. *Luke 14:11* - "For all those who exalt themselves will be humbled, and those who humble themselves will be exalted."

12. *Psalm 18:27* - You save the humble but bring low those whose eyes are haughty.

13. *Proverbs 11:2* - When pride comes, then comes disgrace, but with humility comes wisdom.

14. *Proverbs 22:4* - Humility is the fear of the LORD; its wages are riches and honor and life.

15. *Psalm 25:9* - He guides the humble in what is right and teaches them his way.

16. ***Psalm 55:19*** - God, who is enthroned from of old, who does not change- he will hear them and humble them, because they have no fear of God.

17. ***Psalm 149:4*** - For the Lord takes delight in his people; he crowns the humble with victory.

18. ***1 Peter 5:5*** – In the same way, you who are younger, submit yourselves to your elders. All of you, clothe yourselves with humility toward one another, because, "God opposes the proud but shows favor to the humble"

19. ***Zechariah 9:9*** - Rejoice greatly, Daughter Zion! Shout, Daughter Jerusalem! See, your king comes to you, righteous and victorious, lowly and riding on a donkey, on a colt, the foal of a donkey.

20. ***Mark 10:45*** – "For even the Son of Man did not come to be served, but to serve, and to give his life as a ransom for many."

What Some Great Minds Say About Humility

- The first test of a truly great man is his humility. By humility I don't mean doubt of his powers or hesitation in speaking his opinion, but merely an understanding of the relationship of what he can say and what he can do ~ ***John Ruskin***

- Humility like the darkness, reveals the heavenly lights ~ ***Henry David Thoreau***

- Mental toughness is many things. It is humility because it behooves all of us to remember that simplicity is the sign of greatness and meekness is the sign of true strength. Mental toughness is Spartacism with qualities of sacrifice, self-denial, dedication. It is fearlessness, and it is love ~ ***Vince Lombardi***

- If thou desire the love of God and man, be humble, for the proud heart, as it loves none but itself, is beloved of none but itself. Humility enforces where neither virtue, nor strength, nor reason can prevail ~ ***Francis Quarles***

- There are times God asks us to do things that seem hard. Your flesh will rise and tell you all the reasons why you should put the boat away and not go back out, why you should tell them off and not bite your tongue. This is when you must do like Jesus. Humble yourself so you can become obedient. You have to put your pride down and say, "No, I'm not going to be offended because they left me out. I'm not going to be too proud to ask for forgiveness, to say, 'I'm sorry,' to admit that I was wrong". When we don't have humility, we think we're always right. We'll be stubborn, hard to get along with. Our relationships will be much better if we'll humble ourselves and let somebody else be right ~ ***Joel Osteen***

- Friends, the new beginning, the promotion, the healing, it's in your humility. I'm asking us to put our pride down and start doing what God is asking you to do. Maybe he's asking you to forgive or to treat people better, or like my father, to take a step of faith. Whatever it is, don't talk yourself out of it. May not seem fair. You may not understand it, but if you'll put your pride down and do it anyway, you are setting yourself up for a due time. I believe and declare, because you're humbling exalt you. Like Naaman, you're going to come up out of your seventh dip, where suddenly healing comes, promotion, vindication, freedom, abundance, the fullness of your destiny, in Jesus' name ~ ***Joel Osteen***

- To those people in the huts and villages of half the globe struggling to break the bonds of mass misery, we pledge our best efforts to help them help themselves, for whatever period is required, not because the Communists may be doing it, not because we seek their votes, but because it is right. If a free society cannot help the many who are poor, it cannot save the few who are rich ~ ***John F. Kennedy***

- Mary, my dearest Mother, give me your heart so beautiful, so pure, so immaculate, your heart so full of love and humility, that I may be able to receive Jesus in the Bread of Life, love Him as you loved Him and serve Him in the distressing disguise of the poorest of the poor ~ ***Mother Teresa***

- These are the few ways we can practice humility: To speak as little as possible of one's self. To mind one's own business. Not to want to manage other people's affairs. To avoid curiosity. To accept contradictions and correction cheerfully. To pass over the mistakes of others. To accept insults and injuries. To accept being slighted, forgotten and disliked. To be kind and gentle even under provocation. Never to stand on one's dignity. To choose always the hardest ~ **Mother Teresa**

- Humility is the mother of all virtues; purity, charity and obedience. It is in being humble that our love becomes real, devoted and ardent. If you are humble nothing will touch you, neither praise nor disgrace, because you know what you are. If you are blamed, you will not be discouraged. If they call you a saint, you will not put yourself on a pedestal ~ **Mother Teresa**

- claim to be a simple individual liable to err like any other fellow mortal. I own, however, that I have humility enough to confess my errors and to retrace my steps ~ **Mahatma Gandhi**

- Truth, purity, self-control, firmness, fearlessness, humility, unity, peace, and renunciation - these are the inherent qualities of a civil resister ~ **Mahatma Gandhi**

- We must in strength and humility meet hate with love ~ **Martin Luther King, Jr.**

- We must speak with all the humility that is appropriate to our limited vision, but we must speak ~ **Martin Luther King, Jr.**

- As I have said, the first thing is to be honest with yourself. You can never have an impact on society if you have not changed yourself... Great peacemakers are all people of integrity, of honesty, And humility ~ **Nelson Mandela**

- There is a universal respect and even admiration for those who are humble and simple by nature, and who have absolute confidence in all human beings irrespective of their social status ~ ***Nelson Mandela***

- I have been driven many times upon my knees by the overwhelming conviction that I had nowhere else to go. My own wisdom and that of all about me seemed insufficient for that day ~ ***Abraham Lincoln***

- We have been preserved, these many years, in peace and prosperity. We have grown in numbers, wealth and power, as no other nation has ever grown. But we have forgotten God. We have forgotten the gracious hand which preserved us in peace and multiplied and enriched and strengthened us; and we have vainly imagined, in the deceitfulness of our hearts, that all these blessings were produced by some superior wisdom and virtue of our own. Intoxicated with unbroken success, we have become too self-sufficient to feel the necessity of redeeming and preserving Grace, too proud to pray to the God that made us! ~ ***Abraham Lincoln***

- Humility is simply believing and accepting what God says about us, and God says that we are anything but worthless. Submission is the willingness to give up our right to ourselves, to freely surrender our insistence on having our own way all the time. ~ ***Myles Munroe***

Twelve Ways to Humble Yourself by Billy Graham

1. **Routinely confess your sin to God** *(Luke 18:9-14)*. All of us sin and fall short of the glory of God. However, too few of us have a routine practice of rigorous self-honesty examination. Weekly, even daily, review of our hearts and behaviors, coupled with confession to God, is an essential practice of humility.

2. **Acknowledge your sin to others** *(James 3:2, James 5:16)*. Humility before God is not complete unless there is also humility before man. A true test of our willingness to humble ourselves is willingness to share with others the weaknesses we confess to God. Wisdom, however, dictates that we do so with others that we trust.

3. **Take wrong patiently** *(1 Peter 3:8-17)*. When something is unjust, we want to react and rectify it. However, patiently responding to the unjust accusations and actions of others demonstrates our strength of godly character and provides an opportunity to put on humility.

4. **Actively submit to authority…the good and the bad** *(1 Peter 2:18)*. Our culture does not value submission; rather it promotes individualism. How purposely and actively do you work on submission to those whom God has placed as authorities in your life? Doing so is a good way to humble yourself.

5. **Receive correction and feedback from others graciously** *(Proverbs 10:17, 12:1).* In the Phoenix area, a local East valley pastor was noted for graciously receiving any negative feedback or correction offered. He would simply say "thank you for caring enough to share that with me, I will pray about it and get back to you." Look for the kernel of truth in what people offer you, even if it comes from a dubious source. Always pray, "Lord, what are you trying to show me through this?"

6. **Accept a lowly place** *(Proverbs 25:6,7).* If you find yourself wanting to sit at the head table, wanting others to recognize your contribution or become offended when others are honored or chosen, then pride is present. Purpose to support others being recognized, rather than you. Accept and look for the lowly place; it is the place of humility.

7. **Purposely associate with people of lower state than you** *(Luke 7:36-39).* Jesus was derided by the Pharisees for socializing with the poor and those of lowly state. Our culture is very status conscious and people naturally want to socialize upward. Resist the temptation of being partial to those with status or wealth.

8. **Choose to serve others *(Philippians 1:1, 2 Corinthians 4:5, Matthew 23:11).*** When we serve others, we are serving God's purposes in their lives. Doing so reduces our focus on ourselves and builds the Kingdom of God. When serving another cost us

nothing, we should question whether it is really servanthood

9. **Be quick to forgive** *(Matthew 18: 21-35).* Forgiveness is possibly one of the greatest acts of humility we can do. To forgive is to acknowledge a wrong that has been done us and to further release our right of repayment for the wrong. Forgiveness is denial of self. Forgiveness is not insisting on our way and our justice.

10. **Cultivate a grateful heart** *(1 Thessalonians 5:18).* The more we develop an attitude of gratitude for the gift of salvation and life He has given us, the truer our perspective of self. A grateful heart is a humble heart.

11. **Purpose to speak well of others** *(Ephesians 4:31-32).* Saying negative things about others puts them "one down" and us "one up." Speaking well of others edifies them and builds them up. Make sure, however, that what you say is not intended as flattery.

12. **Treat pride as a condition that always necessitates embracing the cross** *(Luke 9:23).* It is our nature to be proud and it is God's nature in us that brings humility. Committing to a lifestyle of daily dying to ourselves and living through Him is the foundation for true humility.

Math for the Grateful Soul: Gratitude + Humility = Gratihumilitude

Gratihumilitude refers to a display of bravery, modesty, or reverence as a sign of gratitude to Jehovah, God.

Gratefulness
Recognition
Appreciation
Teachability
Intuition
Humbleness
Understanding
Meekness
Infinite love of God
Liberality
Impacting the lives of others in a positive way
Tolerance
Undaunting spirit
Determination
Endurance

Math for the Ungrateful Soul: Humility − Gratitude = Pride

Pride is the quality of having an excessively high opinion of oneself or one's importance. Quality or state of being proud − inordinate self-esteem: "Pride goes before destruction, a haughty spirit before a fall" (***Proverbs 16:18)***. Pride is the opposite of humility. And if Jehovah God encourages us to be humble like his son Jesus Christ, then he cannot like nor encourage pride. God Hates Pride. Pride appears first in the list of seven deadly sins (Pride, greed, lust, envy, gluttony, wrath, and sloth). No vice is more opposed to God. God hates pride because it is a manifestation of the deepest depravity, the root cause of all forms of sin.

What the New International Version of the Holy Bible Says About Pride

1. ***Proverbs 8:13*** ~ To fear the LORD is to hate evil; I hate pride and arrogance, evil behavior and perverse speech.
2. ***Proverbs 11:2*** ~ When pride comes, then comes disgrace, but with humility comes wisdom.
3. ***Proverbs 16:18*** ~ Pride goes before destruction, a haughty spirit before a fall.
4. ***Proverbs 29:23*** ~ Pride brings a person low, but the lowly in spirit gain honor.
5. ***1 John 2:16*** ~ Pride brings a person low, but the lowly in spirit gain honor.

CHAPTER SEVEN: THE VIRTUE OF JUSTICE

What is the Virtue of Justice?

Justness
Uprightness
Sincerity
Trustworthiness
Integrity
Conscience
Equity

Justice is a term used for what is right or "as it should be." Justice is one of God's attributes and flows out of His holiness. Justice and righteousness are often used synonymously in the Bible. Since righteousness is the quality or character of being right or just, it is another attribute of God and incorporates both His justice and holiness. The maintenance or administration of what is just especially by the impartial adjustment of conflicting claims or the assignment of merited rewards or punishments (***Merriam-Webster***).

What the New International Version of the Holy Bible Says About Justice

1. ***Psalms 89:14*** ~ Righteousness and justice are the foundation of your throne; love and faithfulness go before you.
2. ***Ecclesiastes 3:17*** ~ I said to myself, "God will bring into judgment both the righteous and the wicked, for there will be a time for every activity, a time to judge every deed.
3. ***Proverbs 21:15*** ~ When justice is done, it brings joy to the righteous but terror to evildoers.
4. ***Amos 5:24*** ~ But let justice roll on like a river, righteousness like a never-failing stream!
5. ***Zechariah 7:9*** ~ This is what the LORD Almighty said: 'Administer true justice; show mercy and compassion to one another.'
6. ***Isiah 1:17*** ~ Learn to do right; seek justice. Defend the oppressed. Take up the cause of the fatherless; plead the case of the widow.
7. ***Isiah 30:18*** ~ Yet the LORD longs to be gracious to you; therefore, he will rise to show you compassion. For the LORD is a God of justice. Blessed are all who wait for him!
8. ***Hebrews 10:30*** ~ For we know him who said, "It is mine to avenge; I will repay," and again, "The LORD will judge his people."

9. *Hosea 12:6* ~But you must return to your God; maintain love and justice and wait for your God always.

10. *Job 12:22* ~ He reveals the deep things of darkness and brings utter darkness into the light.

11. *2 Peter 3:13* ~ But in keeping with his promise we are looking forward to a new heaven and a new earth, where righteousness dwells.

What Some Great Minds Say About Justice

⋏ The good you do today may be forgotten tomorrow. Do good anyway. Give the world the best you have, and it may never be enough. Give your best anyway. For you see, in the end, it is between you and God. It was never between you and them anyway ~ ***Mother Teresa***

⋏ Justice will not be served until those who are unaffected are as outraged as those who are. ~ ***Benjamin Franklin***

⋏ The arc of the moral universe is long, but it bends towards justice. ~***Theodore Parker***

⋏ I have always found that mercy bears richer fruits than strict justice. ~ ***Abraham Lincoln***

⋏ Where justice is denied, where poverty is enforced, where ignorance prevails, and where any one class is made to feel that society is an organized conspiracy to oppress, rob and degrade them, neither persons nor property will be safe. ~ ***Frederick Douglass***

▲ Human progress is neither automatic nor inevitable... Every step toward the goal of justice requires sacrifice, suffering, and struggle; the tireless exertions and passionate concern of dedicated individuals. ~ **Martin Luther King Jr.**

▲ Being good is easy, what is difficult is being just. ~ ***Victor Hugo***

▲ True peace is not merely the absence of war, it is the presence of justice. ~ ***Jane Addams***

▲ Knowledge which is divorced from justice may be called cunning rather than wisdom. ~ **Marcus Tullius Cicero**

▲ Hebrew word for "charity" tzedakah, simply means "justice" and as this suggests, for Jews, giving to the poor is no optional extra but an essential part of living a just life. ~ ***Peter Singer***

Math for the Grateful Soul: Gratitude + Justice = Gratijustitude

Gratijustitude refers to a demonstration of fairness, honesty, or righteousness in all dealings with others as a sign of gratitude to Jehovah God.

Math for the Ungrateful Soul: Justice – Gratitude = Injustice

Injustice refers to the lack of fairness or justice. The word of God as written in the holy Bible has a lot to say about injustice. We know that God is in favor of justice; consequently, he is against injustice, even in the most basic terms. The writer of Proverbs Solomon mentions this in **Proverbs 20:23**. "The LORD detests differing weights, and dishonest scales do not please him" As long as poverty, injustice and gross inequality persist in our world, none of us can truly rest (**Nelson Mandela**). "Injustice anywhere is a threat to justice everywhere. We are caught in an inescapable network of mutuality, tied in a single garment of destiny. Whatever affects one directly, affects all indirectly." (**Martin Luther King Jr.**)

What the New Version of the Holy Bible Says about Injustice

1. **2 Chronicles 19:7** ~ Now let the fear of the LORD be on you. Judge carefully, for with the LORD our God there is no injustice or partiality or bribery.
2. **Job 6:29** ~ Relent, do not be unjust; reconsider, for my integrity is at stake.
3. **Job 11:14** ~ if you put away the sin that is in your hand and allow no evil to dwell in your tent,

4. ***Proverbs 16:8*** ~Better a little with righteousness than much gain with injustice.

5. ***Ezekiel 18:24*** ~ But if a righteous person turns from their righteousness and commits sin and does the same detestable things the wicked person does, will they live? None of the righteous things that person has done will be remembered. Because of the unfaithfulness they are guilty of and because of the sins they have committed, they will die.

6. ***Romans 9:14*** ~ What then shall we say? Is God unjust? Not at all

7. ***Isaiah 58:6*** ~ Is not this the kind of fasting I have chosen: to loose the chains of injustice and untie the cords of the yoke, to set the oppressed free and break every yoke?

8. ***Micah 6:8*** ~ He has shown you, O mortal, what is good. And what does the LORD require of you? To act justly and to love mercy and to walk humbly with your God.

CHAPTER EIGHT: THE VIRTUE OF PATIENCE

What is the Virtue of Patience?

Product of self-control
Allows believers to grow
Tolerance
Integrity
Endurance
Not giving up
Capacity to accept or tolerate delay or suffering without getting angry or upset
Endurance

What the New International Version of the Holy Bible Says about Patience

1. ***Romans 15:4-6***: "For everything that was written in the past was written to teach us, so that through the endurance taught in the Scriptures and the encouragement they provide we might have hope" (Patience originates from God).

2. ***Galatians 5:22***: "But the fruit of the Spirit is love, joy, peace, forbearance, kindness, goodness, faithfulness" (Patience is part of the fruit of the Spirit)

3. *2 Peter 1:6:* "And to knowledge, self-control; and to self-control, perseverance; and to perseverance, godliness" (Patience is a product of self-control and is part of Godliness)

4. *Matthew 27:14:* But Jesus made no reply, not even to a single charge—to the great amazement of the governor" (Patience was demonstrated by Christ)

5. *Romans 5:4* "And patience produces character, and character produces hope" (Patience helps us grow during trials)

6. *Psalms 27:14:* "Wait for the LORD, be strong and take heart and wait for the LORD" (Patience allows us to be strengthened and blessed by God)

7. *Ecclesiastes 7:8:* "The end of a matter is better than its beginning, and patience is better than pride" (Patience is pleasing to God)

What Some Great Minds Say About Patience

- Each life is made up of mistakes and learning, waiting and growing, practicing patience and being persistent~ **Billy Graham**
- I believe that a trusting attitude and a patient attitude go hand in hand. You see, when you let go and learn to trust God, it releases joy in your life. And when you trust God, you're able to be more patient. Patience is

not just about waiting for something... it's about how you wait, or your attitude while waiting ~*Joyce Meyer*

▲ "Without patience, we will learn less in life. We will see less. We will feel less. We will hear less. Ironically, rush and more usually mean less." ~ ***Mother Teresa***

▲ "Every great dream begins with a dreamer. Always remember, you have within you the strength, the patience, and the passion to reach for the stars to change the world." ~ ***Harriet Tubman***

▲ "Patience is the Companion of Wisdom." ~ ***Augustine of Hippo***

▲ "He that can have patience can have what he will." ~ ***Benjamin Franklin***

▲ "Patience is bitter, but its fruit is sweet." — *Aristotle*

▲ "Patience is power. Patience is not an absence of action; rather it is "timing "it waits on the right time to act, for the right principles and in the right way." — ***Fulton J. Sheen***

▲ "Why is patience so important?" "Because it makes us pay attention." — **Paulo Coelho**

▲ "Faith and patience go hand in hand. When we have faith, it's easier to be patient because we know God is faithful to His promises. Patience is a fruit of the spirit which means that the more we yield ourselves to God, the more patience will rise in our hearts." —*Joel Osteen*

Math for the Grateful Soul: Gratitude + Patience = Gratipatienitude

Gratipatienitude refers to the practice of forgiveness and show of mercy to others as a sign of gratitude to Jehovah God.

Product of self-control
Allows believers to grow
Tolerance
Integrity
Endurance
Not giving up
Capacity to accept or tolerate delay or suffering without getting angry or upset

Math for the Ungrateful Soul: Patience – Gratitude = Wrath

Wrath is strong vengeful anger or indignation.

What the New International Version of the Bible Says About Wrath

1. *Ephesians 4:31* - Get rid of all bitterness, rage and anger, brawling and slander, along with every form of malice.
2. *James 1:19-20* – "My dear brothers and sisters, take note of this: Everyone should be quick to listen, slow to speak and slow to become angry, because human

anger does not produce the righteousness that God desires."

3. ***Proverbs 14:29*** – "Whoever is patient has great understanding, but one who is quick-tempered displays folly."

4. ***Proverbs 15:1*** - "A gentle answer turns away wrath, but a harsh word stirs up anger."

5. ***Proverbs 16:32*** – "Better a patient person than a warrior, one with self-control than one who takes a city."

6. ***Proverbs 19:19*** – "A hot-tempered person must pay the penalty; rescue them, and you will have to do it again."

7. ***Psalm 37:8*** - "Refrain from anger and turn from wrath; do not fret-it leads only to evil."

CHAPTER NINE: THE VIRTUE OF PRUDENCE

What is the Virtue of Prudence?

Paul's Wisdom
Rachel's judiciousness
Ulam's common sense
David's foresight
Ezekiel's shrewdness
Nahum's far-sightedness
Christ's cautiousness
Enoch's advisability

Prudence is the ability to govern and discipline oneself using reason. It means conducting oneself in a **careful and sensible** way. It means paying attention not only to ones needs but to other's needs as well. Prudence means using **sound judgement**. How we get and use prudence in our lives, is by experiences of everyday life. God gives us all common sense, and the bible remains a crucial road map to survival on this temporary habitat called earth.

What the New International Version of the Bible Says about Prudence

1. ***Amos 5:13*** - "Therefore at such a time the prudent person keeps silent, for it is an evil time."
2. ***Mathew 10:16*** - "I am sending you out like sheep among wolves. Therefore, be as shrewd as snakes and as innocent as doves."
3. ***Proverbs 8:12*** – "I, wisdom, dwell together with **prudence;** I possess knowledge and discretion."
4. ***Proverbs 12:16*** - "Fools show their annoyance at once, but the prudent overlook an insult."
5. ***Proverbs 13:16*** - "All who are prudent act with knowledge, but fools expose their folly."
6. ***Proverbs 14:1*** – "The wise woman builds her house, but with her own hands the foolish one tears hers down."
7. ***Proverbs 14 :15*** - "The simple believe anything, but the prudent give thought to their steps."
8. ***Proverbs 15:5*** – "A fool spurns a parent's discipline, but whoever heeds correction shows prudence."
9. ***Proverbs 27:12*** – "The prudent see danger and take refuge, but the simple keep going and pay the penalty."
10. ***Proverbs 31:26*** – "She speaks with wisdom, and faithful instruction is on her tongue."

What Some Great Minds Say About Prudence

- "Prudence does not mean failing to accept responsibilities and postponing decisions; it means being committed to making joint decisions after pondering responsibly the road to be taken." --- ***Pope Benedict XVI***
- "Prudence is not only the first in rank of the virtues political and moral, but she is the director and regulator, the standard of them all" --- ***Edmund Burke***
- "Prudence is the virtue by which we discern what is proper to do under various circumstances in time and place." --- ***John Milton***
- "An ounce of prevention is worth a pound of cure." ~ ***Benjamin Franklin***
- "Prudence is the knowledge of things to be sought, and those to be shunned." ~***Marcus Tullius Cicero***
- "Prudence is foresight and far-sightedness. It's the ability to make immediate decisions on the basis of their longer-range effects." ~***John Ortberg***

Math for the Grateful Soul: Gratitude + Prudence = Gratiprudenitude

Gratiprudenitude refers to the use of reason in governing and disciplining oneself as a sign of gratitude to Jehovah God.

Gratefulness
Recognition
Appreciation
Teachability
Intuition
Product of self-control
Allows believers to grow
Tolerance
Integrity
Endurance
Not giving up
Impacting the lives of others in a positive way
Tolerance
Undaunting spirit
Determination
Endurance

Math for the Ungrateful Soul: Prudence – Gratitude = Folly.

Folly is a foolish act, idea, practice, lack of good sense; foolishness. Show gratitude to Jehovah God by avoiding foolish acts that do not glorify God.

What the New International Version of the Holy Bible Says About Folly

1. *1 Corinthians 1:18*: For the word of the cross is foolishness to those who are perishing, but to **us who are being saved it is the power of God**

2. ***Genesis 34:7***: And the sons of Jacob came out of the field when they heard it: and the men were grieved, and they were very wroth, because he had wrought folly in Israel in lying with Jacob's daughter: which thing ought not to be done.

3. ***Jeremiah 10*:18**: But they are altogether stupid and foolish in their discipline of delusion--their idol is wood!

4. ***Jeremiah 10*:21**: For the shepherds have become stupid and have not sought the LORD; Therefore, they have not prospered, and all their flock is scattered.

5. ***I Samuel 13*:13**: Samuel said to Saul, "You have acted foolishly; you have not kept the commandment of the LORD your God, which He commanded you, for now the LORD would have established your kingdom over Israel forever."

CHAPTER TEN: THE VIRTUE OF TEMPERANCE

What is the Virtue of Temperance?

Timothy's self-control
Elijah's self-restraint
Moses's self-discipline
Pharaoh's self-mastery
Enoch's self-possession
Rehab's single-mindedness
Abigail's determination
Naomi's steadfastness
Christ's resoluteness
Eve's untaintedness

The Holy Bible defines Temperance as being able to master your own desires and passions – to not be puppeteer by your peers, by the world's fads, or by your own desires and passions (Romans 12: 1-2) Temperance is the nurse of chastity (William Wyshele)

As described by Fritz Chery, the word temperance is used in the **King James Version** of the Bible and it means self-control. Many times, when used temperance refers to alcohol, but it can be used for anything. It can be for **caffeine consumption, gluttony, thoughts**, etc. By ourselves we have no self-control, but temperance is one of the fruits of the Spirit. The Holy Spirit helps us with self-control, overcoming sin, and obeying the Lord. Submit to the Lord. Continually cry out to God for help. You know the area you need help with. Don't say you want to change, but just remain there. In your walk of faith, you will need self-discipline. To have victory over your temptations you must walk by the Spirit and not the flesh.

What the New International Version of the Holy Bible Says About Temperance

1. *Acts 24:25* – "As Paul talked about righteousness, self-control and the judgment to come, Felix was afraid and said, "That's enough for now! You may leave. When I find it convenient, I will send for you."
2. *1 Corinthians 6:19-20* – "Do you not know that your bodies are temples of the Holy Spirit, who is in you, whom you have received from God? You are not your own; you were bought at a price. Therefore, honor God with your bodies."
3. *1 Corinthians 9:27* – "No, I strike a blow to my body and make it my slave so that after I have preached to others, I myself will not be disqualified for the prize."
4. *Colossians 3:10* – "And have put on the new self, which is being renewed in knowledge in the image of its Creator."
5. *Ephesians 5:18* – "And be not drunk with wine, wherein is excess; but be filled with the Spirit;"

6. *Galatians 5:19-21* – "The acts of the flesh are obvious: sexual immorality, impurity and debauchery; idolatry and witchcraft; hatred, discord, jealousy, fits of rage, selfish ambition, dissensions, factions and envy; drunkenness, orgies, and the like. I warn you, as I did before, that those who live like this will not inherit the kingdom of God."

7. *Galatians 5: 22 -24* – "The fruit of the Spirit is love, joy, peace, forbearance, kindness, goodness, faithfulness, gentleness and self-control. Against such things there is no law. Those who belong to Christ Jesus have crucified the flesh with its passions and desires."

8. *2 Peter 1:5-6* – "For this very reason, make every effort to add to your faith goodness; and to goodness, knowledge; and to knowledge, self-control; and to self-control, perseverance; and to perseverance, godliness;

9. *Philippians 4:5-9* – "Let your gentleness be evident to all. The LORD is near. Do not be anxious about anything, but in every situation, by prayer and petition, with thanksgiving, present your requests to God. And the peace of God, which transcends all understanding, will guard your hearts and your minds in Christ Jesus. Finally, brothers and sisters, whatever is true, whatever is noble, whatever is right, whatever is pure, whatever is lovely, whatever is admirable-if anything is excellent or praiseworthy-think about such things. Whatever you have learned or received

or heard from me or seen in me-put it into practice. And the God of peace will be with you."

10. ***Philippians 4:10-13*** – "But I rejoiced in the Lord greatly that now at last your care for me has flourished again; though you surely did care, but you lacked opportunity. Not that I speak regarding the need, for I have learned in whatever state I am, to be content: I know how to be abased, and I know how to abound. Everywhere and in all things, I have learned both to be full and to be hungry, both to abound and to suffer need. I can do all things through Christ who strengthens me."

11. ***Proverbs 25:16*** - "If you find honey, eat just enough- too much of it, and you will vomit."

12. ***Proverbs 25:28*** – "Like a city whose walls are broken through is a person who lacks self-control."

13. ***Proverbs 31:4-5*** – "It is not for kings, Lemuel- it is not for kings to drink wine, not for rulers to crave beer, lest they drink and forget what has been decreed, and deprive all the oppressed of their rights."

14. ***Romans 8:26*** – "In the same way, the Spirit helps us in our weakness. We do not know what we ought to pray for, but the Spirit himself intercedes for us through wordless groans."

15. ***Romans 12: 1-2*** – "Therefore, I urge you, brothers and sisters, in view of God's mercy, to offer your bodies as a living sacrifice, holy and pleasing to God- this is your true and proper So then, let us not be

like others, who are asleep, but let us be awake and sober. For those who sleep, sleep at night, and those who get drunk, get drunk at night. But since we belong to the day, let us be sober, putting on faith and love as a breastplate, and the hope of salvation as a helmet. Worship. Do not conform to the pattern of this world but be transformed by the renewing of your mind. Then you will be able to test and approve what God's will is-his good, pleasing and perfect will."

16. Romans 13:14 – "Rather, clothe yourselves with the LORD Jesus Christ, and do not think about how to gratify the desires of the flesh."

17. 1 Thessalonians 5:6-8 - "So then, let us not be like others, who are asleep, but let us be awake and sober. For those who sleep, sleep at night, and those who get drunk, get drunk at night. But since we belong to the day, let us be sober, putting on faith and love as a breastplate, and the hope of salvation as a helmet."

18. 1 Thessalonians 5:21 - "but test them all; hold on to what is good,"

19. 1 Timothy 3:8-9 "In the same way, deacons are to be worthy of respect, sincere, not indulging in much wine, and not pursuing dishonest gain. They must keep hold of the deep truths of the faith with a clear conscience."

20. Titus 2:12 - "It teaches us to say "No" to ungodliness and worldly passions, and to live self-controlled, upright and godly lives in this present age,"

What Some Great Minds Say About Temperance

- None seemed to think the injury arose from the use of a bad thing but from the abuse of a very good thing ~ *Abraham Lincoln*
- Temperance is the first virtue that perfects man's ability to act well with one's self from within one's self ~ *Doug McManaman*
- Temperance takes the needs of this life, as the rule of the pleasurable objects of which it makes use, and uses them only for as much as the need of this life requires ~ *Doug McManaman*
- There is no difference between knowledge and temperance; for he who knows what is good and embraces it, who knows what is bad and avoids it, is learned and temperate ~ *Socrates*
- Lost wealth may be replaced by industry, lost knowledge by study, lost health by temperance or medicine, but lost time is gone forever ~ *Samuel Smiles*
- Temperance is moderation in the things that are good and total abstinence from the things that are foul ~ *Frances E. Willard*
- Temperance puts wood on the fire, meal in the barrel, flour in the tub, money in the purse, credit in the country, contentment in the house, clothes on the back, and vigor in the body ~ *Benjamin Franklin*

- Exercise and temperance can preserve something of our early strength even in old age ~ **Marcus Tullius Cicero**
- The whole duty of man is embraced in the two principles of abstinence and patience: temperance in prosperity, and patient courage in adversity ~ **Seneca the Younger**
- The ingredients of health and long life, are great temperance, open air, easy labor, and little care ~ **Philip Sidney**
- Temperance is simply a disposition of the mind which binds the passion ~ **Thomas Aquinas**
- Temperance is a tree which as for its root very little contentment, and for its fruit calm and peace ~ **Gautama Buddha**
- A man who is eating or lying with his wife or preparing to go to sleep in humility, thankfulness and temperance, is, by Christian standards, in an infinitely higher state than one who is listening to Bach or reading Plato in a state of pride ~ **C.S. Lewis**
- Thirteen virtues necessary for true success: temperance, silence, order, resolution, frugality, industry, sincerity, justice, moderation, cleanliness, tranquility, chastity, and humility ~ **Benjamin Franklin**
- Temperance is the wisdom to know that not every constructive job requires a hammer ~ **Wes Fesler**

- Finish each day before you begin the next and interpose a solid wall of sleep between the two. This you cannot do without temperance ~ **Ralph Waldo Emerson**

- The virtue of prosperity is temperance; the virtue of adversity is fortitude ~ **Francis Bacon**

- Temperance and labor are the two best physicians of man; labor sharpens the appetite, and temperance prevents from indulging to excess ~ **Jean-Jacques Rousseau**

- For both excessive and insufficient exercise destroy one's strength, and both eating and drinking too much or too little destroy health, whereas the right quantity produces, increases and preserves it. So, it is the same with temperance, courage and the other virtues. This much then, is clear: in all our conduct it is the mean that is to be commended ~ **Aristotle**

- Temperance keeps the senses clear and unembarrassed and makes them seize the object with more keenness and satisfaction. It appears with life in the face, and decorum in the person; it gives you the command of your head, and secures your health, and preserves you in a condition for business ~ **Jeremy Collier**

- Temperance is corporeal piety; it is the preservation of divine order in the body ~ **Theodore Parker**

Math for the Grateful Soul: Gratitude + Temperance= Gratitemperitude

Gratitemperitude refers to the exercise of compassion and equanimity towards others as a sign of gratitude to Jehovah God.

God's gracefulness
Rehab's single-mindedness
Abel's appreciation
Timothy's modesty
Isaac's intuition
Tolerance of Daniel
Elijah's self-restraint
Moses's self-discipline
Pharaoh's self-mastery
Enoch's self-possession
Rachel's compassion
Integrity of Samuel
Timothy's tolerance
Undaunting spirit of Job
David's determination
Eve's untaintedness

Math for the Ungrateful Soul: Temperance − Gratitude = Gluttony.

Gluttony is the over-indulgence and over-consumption of food, drink, or wealth to the point of extravagance or waste.

Gluttony is insensibility towards the pleasures of life. Gluttony is a sign of ingratitude to Jehovah God.

What the New International Version of the Holy Bible Says About Gluttony

1. ***1 Corinthians 3:16-17***: Don't you know that you yourselves are God's temple and that God's Spirit dwells in your midst? If anyone destroys God's temple, God will destroy that person; for God's temple is sacred, and you together are that temple.
2. ***Ephesians 5:18***: Do not get drunk on wine, which leads to debauchery. Instead, be filled with the Spirit,
3. ***Philippians 3:18-19***: For, as I have often told you before and now tell you again even with tears, many live as enemies of **the** cross of Christ. Their destiny is destruction, their god is their stomach, and their glory is in their shame. Their mind is set on earthly things.
4. ***Proverbs 23:2-3:*** And put a knife to your throat if you are given to gluttony. Do not crave his delicacies, for that food is deceptive.
5. ***Proverbs 23:4:*** Don't wear yourself out trying to get rich. Be wise enough to know when to quit.

CONCLUSION
SHOW GRATITUDE FOR THE UPLIFTING GRACE OF GOD!!!!!!!!!

Gratitude facilitates all other virtues and the uplifting Grace of God is an undeserved favor from Jehovah God to humanity without humanity doing anything to earn or merit it. It is but humbling to receive God's uplifting Grace with an attitude of gratitude. Grace is not empowerment, but it produces empowerment. An attitude of gratitude will enable you see hope where others see Destruction. However, serendipity is different from grace. Grace is unmerited favor it cannot and should never be redefined, it's already established.

Serendipity is when God gives you a blessing in an unexpected way and in an unexpected place. Serendipity does not come from Latin or Greek, but rather was created by a British nobleman in the mid-1700s from an ancient Persian fairy tale. The meaning of the word, good luck in finding valuable things unintentionally, refers to the fairy tale characters who were always making discoveries through chance.

Nelson Mandela goes down in history as one of the 20th century recipients of Jehovah God's amazing Grace. His gift of Grace had an effect that transformed south Africa and many other nations and individuals. By finding his freedom in grace and dignity, he was able to help bring freedom to all South Africans (The Christian Science Monitor). The

Luminary Nelson Mandela did not take Jehovah God's Grace upon his life for granted. He wrote in a letter to his wife from his Robben Island prison cell in 1975, the qualities that are crucial for anyone – honesty, sincerity, simplicity, humility, pure generosity, absence of vanity, readiness to serve others – "are within easy reach of every soul." His fellow South African, Archbishop Desmond Tutu, says Mandela's grace and passion came from knowing "the infinite worth of everyone because of being created in the image of God." Such understanding was behind his many symbolic acts of healing. Nelson Mandela believed and preached that no one is born hating another person because of the color of his skin, or his background, or his religion. People must learn to hate, and if they can learn to hate, they can be taught to love, for love comes more naturally to the human heart than its opposite.

Only the grace of God can give you land you did not work for and cities you didn't build. Grace therefore is the undisputed evidence of Jehovah God's mighty presence and his goodness that can enable you bloom wherever you are planted.

Grace that connects with virtue is called the uplifting grace of Jehovah God.

God's Love for us
Reaching us whenever and totally undeserved
According to his riches and glory
Contained in his word, the holy Bible
Everlasting and permanently irrevocable

What the New International Version of the Bible Says About Grace

1. ***Titus 2:11 &12***: "For the grace of God has appeared, bringing salvation for all people. Grace teaches us to renounce ungodliness and worldly passions, and to live a sensible, upright, and godly life in the present age"

2. ***Romans 12:1&2***: "So, I appeal to you brethren, by the mercies of God —present your bodies as a living sacrifice, holy and acceptable to God. This is your reasonable service. Don't be conformed to this world. Rather be transformed by the renewal of your mind. Then you will prove what the will of God is — what is good and acceptable and perfect."

3. ***Romans 6:1&2***: "So what shall we say? Should we continue in sin that grace may abound? No way! How can we who died to sin still live in sin?2

4. ***Romans 6:12&13***: "So, don't let sin reign in your mortal body, to make you obey its lusts. Don't present your members to sin as instruments for unrighteousness. Rather, present yourselves to God as those who have been brought from death to life. Offer the members of your body to God as instruments for righteousness"

5. ***Romans 6:14***: "If you do that, sin will have no dominion over you, since you are not under law but under grace"

6. *2 Peter 1:2 &3*: "May grace and peace be multiplied to you in the knowledge of God and of Jesus our Lord. His divine power has granted to us all things that pertain to life and godliness. Those blessings were given through the knowledge of him who called us to his own glory and excellence"

7. *2 Peter 1:4*: "Our Lord has granted us his precious and magnificent promises. Through them, you were able to become partakers of the divine nature as you escaped the corruption that's in the world through lust."

8. *2 Peter 1:5-7*: "For this very reason, make every effort to add virtue to your faith. To virtue, add knowledge. To knowledge, add self-control. To self-control, add steadfastness. To steadfastness, add godliness. To godliness, add brotherly kindness. To brotherly kindness, add love."

9. *2 Peter 1:8 & 9*: "For if these qualities are yours and are increasing, you won't be idle or unfruitful in the knowledge of our Lord Jesus Christ. But if you lack these qualities, you are so nearsighted as to be blind. You have forgotten that you were cleansed from your former sins."

10. *2Peter 1:10 &11*: "So rather brethren, be more diligent to ensure your calling and election. For if you practice these qualities, you will never fall. In this way there will be richly provided for you an entrance into the eternal kingdom of our Lord and Savior Jesus Christ."

11. ***Romans 12:6***: We have different gifts, according to the grace given to each of us. If your gift is prophesying, then prophesy in accordance with your faith;

12. ***Genesis 39: 2-6***: "And the Lord was with Joseph, and he was a prosperous man; and he was in the house of his master the Egyptian. And his master saw that the Lord was with him, and that the Lord made all that he did to prosper in his hand. And Joseph found grace in his sight, and he served him: and he made him overseer over his house, and all that he had he put into his hand. And it came to pass from the time that he had made him overseer in his house, and over all that he had, that the Lord blessed the Egyptian's house for Joseph's sake; and the blessing of the Lord was upon all that he had in the house, and in the field. And he left all that he had in Joseph's hand; and he knew not ought he have, save the bread which he did eat. And Joseph was a goodly person, and well favored."

13. ***Ephesians 2:8***; "For it is by grace you have been saved, through faith—and this is not from yourselves, it is the gift of God"

14. ***1 Peter 3:7***; "Husbands, in the same way be considerate as you live with your wives and treat them with respect as the weaker partner and as heirs with you of the gracious gift of life, so that nothing will hinder your prayers."

15. ***1 Peter 5:5-7***; "In the same way, you who are younger, submit yourselves to your elders. All of you,

clothe yourselves with humility toward one another, because, God opposes the proud but shows favor to the humble. Humble yourselves, therefore, under God's mighty hand, that he may lift you up in due time. Cast all your anxiety on him because he cares for you."

16. ***1Peter 4:10-11:*** "Each of you should use whatever gift you have received to serve others, as faithful stewards of God's grace in its various forms. If anyone speaks, they should do so as one who speaks the very words of God. If anyone serves, they should do so with the strength God provides, so that in all things God may be praised through Jesus Christ. To him be the glory and the power for ever and ever. Amen."

17. ***Romans 12:6 & 7:*** "We have different gifts, according to the grace given to each of us. If your gift is prophesying, then prophesy in accordance with your faith;"

What the Luminary Dr. Mensah Otabil Says About Grace

- Grace is God's character by which he shows himself compassionate to us.
- Grace is God's Goodwill towards us.
- Grace is God's willingness to share in our lives.
- Grace is God's help extended to us.
- Grace makes God to stand with us when we are weak.

- The New testament starts with Grace; the laws were handed to Moses, but Grace came through Jesus Christ.
- Faith cannot operate without Grace, for when Grace provides, faith receives (Ephesians 2:8).
- A proud spirit will hinder the Grace of God (1 Peter 5:5-7).
- An atmosphere of bitterness and insensitivity will hinder the Grace of God (1 Peter 3:7).
- The Grace of God is hindered when you devalue what you have been blessed with.
- Talents are God's grace at work in us (1Peter 4:10-11), (Romans 12:6&7).

What Some Great Minds Say About God's Uplifting Grace

- "Grace isn't a little prayer you chant before receiving a meal. It's a way to live. The law tells me how crooked I am. Grace comes along and straightens me out." ~ **Dwight Lyman Moody**
- "Grace is free sovereign favor to the ill-deserving." ~ **Benjamin B. Warfield**
- "The grace of the spirit comes only from heaven and lights up the whole bodily presence." ~ **Charles Haddon Spurgeon**
- "Abounding sin is the terror of the world, but abounding grace is the hope of mankind." ~ **A. W. Tozer**

- "For grace is given not because we have done good works, but in order that we may be able to do them." ~*Saint Augustine Of Hippo*
- "Grace is the love that gives, that loves the unlovely and the unlovable." ~ *Oswald C. Hoffmann*
- "Grace comes into the soul, as the morning sun into the world; first a dawning, then a light; and at last the sun in his full and excellent brightness." ~*Thomas Adams*
- "The law detects, grace alone conquers sin." ~*Saint Augustine Of Hippo*
- "You must pay for everything in this world one way and another. There is nothing free except the Grace of God. You cannot earn that or deserve it." ~ *Charles Portis*
- "When grace moves in... guilt moves out." ~ *Max Lucado*
- "Only those who are truly aware of their sin can truly cherish grace." ~*C.J. Mahaney*
- "If I'm not showing grace . . . have I forgotten the grace I've been shown" ~ *John F. Macarthur Jr.*
- "Grace is available for each of us every day - our spiritual daily bread - but we've got to remember to ask for it with a grateful heart and not worry about whether there will be enough for tomorrow." ~ *Sarah Ban Breathnach*
- "What gives me the most hope every day is God's grace; knowing that his grace is going to give me the

strength for whatever I face, knowing that nothing is a surprise to God." ~ ***Rick Warren***

- "The meaning of life. The wasted years of life. The poor choices of life. God answers the mess of life with one word: 'grace." ***Max Lucado***

- "Amazing grace! (how sweet the sound) That saved a wretch like me! I once was lost, but now am found, was blind, but now I see. ~ ***John Newton***

- "That is the mystery of grace: it never comes too late." ~ ***François Mauriac***

- "We cannot "psychologize" the grace of God. God's actions are outside and above our human sciences." ~ ***John Powell***

- "Grace means undeserved kindness. It is the gift of God to man the moment he sees he is unworthy of God's favor." ~ ***Dwight L. Moody***

- "Grace is the voice that calls us to change and then gives us the power to pull it off." ~ ***Max Lucado***

- "Grace is not simply leniency when we have sinned. Grace is the enabling gift of God not to sin. Grace is power, not just pardon." ~ ***John Piper***

- "Your worst days are never so bad that you are beyond the reach of God's grace. And your best days are never so good that you are beyond the need of God's grace." ~ ***Jerry Bridges***

- "Grace... expresses two complementary thoughts: God's unmerited favor to us through Christ, and God's divine assistance to us through the Holy Spirit." ~ ***Jerry Bridges***

- "Grace can neither be bought, earned, or won by the creature. If it could be, it would cease to be grace." ~ ***Arthur W. Pink***
- "Grace is the very opposite of merit... Grace is not only undeserved favor, but it is favor, shown to the one who has deserved the very opposite." ~ ***Harry Ironside***

An attitude of gratitude will enable God's uplifting grace to take you from a follower to a leader and from a leader to an agent of change;

- Be strong in God's Grace
- Grace will show you who you are
- Grace will show you where you came from
- Grace will show you where you are heading to
- Grace will reveal your Godly ordained purpose

Brethren's, God's uplifting Grace is sufficient, thus, with an attitude of gratitude, be strong in God's Grace. Amen

REVIEWS

God will tell me who you really are as I continue to search the source of your wisdom. Ride on and pull us along. You have given me all assurance that everything comes at the appointed time. I am glad you speak a language that I understand so well. Go and do His work daughter of the Almighty.

~Mrs. Forchu Florence Asafor (AKA, Mummy Flo,)

Amazing book. I pray that everyone will receive a blessing and a greater understanding on Gratitude.

~ Dr. Donna Daniels.

www.ingramcontent.com/pod-product-compliance
Lightning Source LLC
Chambersburg PA
CBHW072028110526
44592CB00012B/1431